THE CHRISTMAS COOKIE
COOKBOOK

13-Digit ISBN: 978-1-64643-038-3
10-Digit ISBN: 1-64643-038-7

This book may be ordered by mail from the publisher. Please include $5.99 for postage and handling. Please support your local bookseller first!

Books published by Cider Mill Press Book Publishers are available at special discounts for bulk purchases in the United States by corporations, institutions, and other organizations. For more information, please contact the publisher.

Cider Mill Press Book Publishers
"Where good books are ready for press"
501 Nelson Place
Nashville, Tennessee 37214
cidermillpress.com

Typography: Alternate Gothic Pro No 2, Baskerville

Image Credits: Photos on pages 22 and 181 courtesy of Cider Mill Press. Snowflake and decorative frame illustrations © CreativeMarket.com | Emily Schramm. All other photos used under official license from StockFood and Shutterstock.

Printed in the USA

23 24 25 26 27 VER 11 10 9 8 7

THE CHRISTMAS COOKIE COOKBOOK

Give the Gift of Baking with This
Collection of 100+ Delicious Recipes

CIDER MILL
PRESS

BOOK
PUBLISHERS

CONTENTS

INTRODUCTION: 'TIS THE SEASON FOR COOKIES

The kitchen is the source of the warmth everyone associates with the Christmas season. Thoughts invariably turn toward food the minute December rolls around, a signal to every family member who knows their way around a mixing bowl that their specialties will soon be called for.

Among all of the goodies that have embedded themselves in holiday tradition, none is more treasured than the Christmas cookie. Even Santa Claus, the big man himself, requires plate after plate to go about his all-important duties. From the buttery spritz cookies we turned out at the table with Grandma and her magical cookie press to Dad's famed chocolate truffles we rolled in cocoa powder while standing on a stool, some of our strongest holiday memories seem to revolve around these confections.

We created *The Christmas Cookie Cookbook* and its more than 100 recipes to help you keep these valuable recollections alive—and to help you create new ones. Maybe you want to whip up something special with your children or grandchildren as you all take in *It's a Wonderful Life* or another classic Christmas movie. Perhaps you need a new holiday favorite for that friend or loved one who has gone vegan or gluten-free. Maybe you're looking for a treat that will shine on the dessert table at a party, or one you can fashion to look as festive as it tastes. In the following pages, you will find recipes tailored to these instances and many more. With each new creation, may you put smile after smile on the faces of your loved ones and capture exactly what the Christmas season should be—a time of togetherness and simple pleasures.

You already know that this is the most wonderful time of the year—but you may be surprised how much more wonderful it can be with *The Christmas Cookie Cookbook* in hand.

CLASSICS

From the pleasant spice of gingerbread to the crisp sweetness of a
frosted sugar cookie, all of the
holiday cookie cornerstones can
be found right here.

GINGERBREAD COOKIES

YIELD: 24 COOKIES | ACTIVE TIME: 25 MINUTES | TOTAL TIME: 2 HOURS

1 stick unsalted butter, at room temperature

⅔ cup firmly packed dark brown sugar

2 large eggs

3½ tablespoons molasses

4 cups all-purpose flour, plus more for dusting

2 teaspoons ground ginger

½ teaspoon cinnamon

¼ teaspoon ground cloves

½ teaspoon grated nutmeg

1½ teaspoons baking soda

½ teaspoon kosher salt

1 cup confectioners' sugar, plus 2 tablespoons

1 tablespoon milk

Food coloring, for decoration

Preferred candies, for decoration

1. Place the butter and brown sugar in a mixing bowl and beat at low speed with a handheld mixer fitted with the paddle attachment until pale and fluffy, scraping down the bowl as needed. Add the eggs and molasses, reduce speed to low, and beat to incorporate. Sift the flour, ginger, cinnamon, cloves, nutmeg, baking soda, and salt into a separate mixing bowl. Gradually add the dry mixture to the wet mixture, and beat until the dough just holds together. Form the dough into a ball, cover in plastic wrap, and refrigerate for 1 hour.

2. Remove the dough from the refrigerator and let it come to room temperature. Preheat the oven to 350°F and line two baking sheets with parchment paper. Place ½-cup portions of the dough on a flour-dusted work surface and roll out to ⅛-inch thick. Use cookie cutters to cut the cookies into the desired shapes and place them on the baking sheets.

3. Place in the oven and bake for 10 minutes, until the edges start to brown. Remove from the oven and transfer to wire racks to cool completely.

4. Place the confectioners' sugar and milk in a mixing
   bowl, and stir until the frosting achieves the desired consistency. If using several hues of food coloring, divide
   the frosting between the requisite number of bowls. Add
   the food coloring, stir to incorporate, and transfer each
   color of frosting into its own piping bag fitted with a fine
   tip. Decorate the cookies as desired with the frosting and
   your preferred candies. Let the frosting set before serving.

CHOCOLATE CHIP COOKIES

YIELD: 16 COOKIES | ACTIVE TIME: 15 MINUTES | TOTAL TIME: 45 MINUTES

14 tablespoons unsalted butter

1¾ cups all-purpose flour

½ teaspoon baking soda

½ cup granulated sugar

¾ cup gently packed dark brown sugar

1 teaspoon kosher salt

2 teaspoons pure vanilla extract

1 large egg

1 large egg yolk

1¼ cups semisweet chocolate chips

1. Preheat the oven to 350°F and line two baking sheets with parchment paper. Place the butter in a saucepan and cook over medium-high heat until it is dark brown and has a nutty aroma. Transfer to a heatproof mixing bowl.

2. Place the flour and baking soda in a mixing bowl and whisk until combined. In the bowl containing the melted butter, add the sugars, salt, and vanilla and beat until combined. Add the egg and egg yolk and beat until mixture is smooth and thick.

3. Add the dry mixture and stir until incorporated. Fold in the chocolate chips. Form the mixture into 16 balls and place on the parchment-lined baking sheets. Place one sheet of cookies in the oven at a time. Bake, rotating the sheet halfway through, for about 12 minutes, until the cookies are golden brown. Remove from the oven and briefly let cool on the baking sheet before transferring to a wire rack to cool completely.

FROSTED SUGAR COOKIES

YIELD: 40 COOKIES | ACTIVE TIME: 20 MINUTES | TOTAL TIME: 1 HOUR

2⅔ cups all-purpose flour, plus more for dusting

¾ cup granulated sugar

2 teaspoons vanilla sugar

1 pinch kosher salt

Juice and zest of 1 lemon

2 sticks unsalted butter, divided into tablespoons

1 egg

2 cups confectioners' sugar

Food coloring (optional), for decoration

Decorative sugars (optional), for decoration

1. Place the flour, granulated sugar, vanilla sugar, salt, and lemon zest in a mixing bowl and stir to combine. Add the butter and work the mixture with a pastry blender until incorporated. Add the egg and work the mixture with your hands until a smooth dough forms. Cover the dough with plastic wrap and refrigerate for 30 minutes.

2. Preheat the oven to 375°F and line two baking sheets with parchment paper. Place the dough on a flour-dusted work surface and roll it out to ⅛-inch thick. Cut into desired shapes with cookie cutters and place them on the baking sheets.

3. Place the cookies in the oven and bake for about 10 minutes, until they are golden brown. Remove from the oven and briefly let cool on baking sheets before transferring to wire racks to cool completely.

4. Place the confectioners' sugar and lemon juice in a mixing bowl and stir until the frosting achieves the desired thickness. If desired, add food coloring. Spread the frosting over the biscuits and sprinkle the decorative sugars on top, if desired. Let the frosting set before serving.

OATMEAL RAISIN COOKIES

YIELD: 16 COOKIES | ACTIVE TIME: 20 MINUTES | TOTAL TIME: 1 HOUR

4 tablespoons unsalted butter

¼ teaspoon cinnamon

¾ cup firmly packed dark brown sugar

½ cup granulated sugar

½ cup vegetable oil

1 large egg

1 large egg yolk

1 teaspoon pure vanilla extract

1 cup all-purpose flour

½ teaspoon baking soda

¾ teaspoon kosher salt

3 cups rolled oats

½ cup raisins

1. Preheat the oven to 350°F and line two baking sheets with parchment paper. Place the butter in a skillet and warm over medium-high heat until it is a dark golden brown and has a nutty aroma. Transfer to a mixing bowl and whisk in the cinnamon, brown sugar, granulated sugar, and vegetable oil. When the mixture is combined, add the egg, egg yolk, and vanilla, and whisk until incorporated.

2. Place the flour, baking soda, and salt in a separate mixing bowl and whisk to combine. Gradually add this mixture to the wet mixture and stir until thoroughly combined. Add the oats and raisins, and stir until they are evenly distributed throughout the mixture.

3. Form the dough into 16 balls and place them on the baking sheets. Press down on the balls of dough to flatten them slightly. Place the cookies in the oven and bake for about 10 minutes, until the edges start to brown. Remove from the oven and let cool on the baking sheets for 5 minutes before transferring to wire racks to cool completely.

CORNMEAL COOKIES

YIELD: 24 COOKIES | ACTIVE TIME: 20 MINUTES | TOTAL TIME: 3 HOURS

1 stick unsalted butter

¾ cup confectioners' sugar

1 large egg, at room temperature

½ teaspoon pure vanilla extract

⅔ cup all-purpose flour

¼ cup finely ground cornmeal

2 tablespoons cornstarch

¼ teaspoon kosher salt

1. Place the butter and sugar in a mixing bowl and beat at medium speed with a handheld mixer fitted with the paddle attachment until pale and fluffy, scraping down the sides of the bowl as needed. Add the egg and vanilla, reduce speed to low, and beat to incorporate. Gradually incorporate the flour, cornmeal, cornstarch, and salt, and beat until the mixture is a stiff dough.

2. Place the dough on a sheet of parchment paper and roll it into a log that is 2½ inches in diameter. Cover in plastic wrap and refrigerate for 2 hours.

3. Preheat the oven to 350°F and line two baking sheets with parchment paper. Cut the chilled dough into ⅓-inch-thick rounds and arrange the cookies on the baking sheets. Place the cookies in the oven and bake until the edges start to brown, about 10 minutes. Remove from the oven, let cool on the sheets for a few minutes, and then transfer the cookies to wire racks to cool completely.

RASPBERRY PIE BARS

YIELD: 12 TO 24 BARS | ACTIVE TIME: 30 MINUTES | TOTAL TIME: 1 HOUR

2 balls piecrust dough

7 cups fresh raspberries

2 cups granulated sugar, plus more to taste

⅔ cup all-purpose flour

Juice of 1 lemon

1 pinch kosher salt

1 egg, beaten

1. Preheat the oven to 350°F and grease a rimmed 15-by-10-inch baking pan with nonstick cooking spray. Roll out one of the balls of dough so that it fits the pan. Place it in the pan, press down to ensure that it is even, and prick the dough with a fork. Roll out the other ball of dough so that it is slightly larger than the pan.

2. Place the raspberries, sugar, flour, lemon juice, and salt in a mixing bowl and stir until well combined. Spread this mixture evenly across the dough in the baking pan.

3. Place the remaining piece of dough over the filling and trim any excess. Brush the top with the egg and sprinkle with additional sugar. Place in the oven and bake until golden brown, about 40 minutes. Remove from the oven and let cool before slicing.

LEMON SHORTBREAD

YIELD: 30 COOKIES | ACTIVE TIME: 20 MINUTES | TOTAL TIME: 1 HOUR AND 45 MINUTES

2⅔ cups all-purpose flour, plus more for dusting

1 pinch cinnamon

½ teaspoon kosher salt

¾ cup shortening

¾ cup caster sugar

2 small egg yolks

2 teaspoons pure lemon extract

Zest of 1 lemon

1½ cups almond meal

Confectioners' sugar, for dusting

1. Place the flour, cinnamon, and salt in a large mixing bowl and stir to combine. Place the shortening and caster sugar in a separate mixing bowl and beat at medium speed with a handheld mixer fitted with the paddle attachment until pale and fluffy, scraping down the sides of the bowl as needed. Add the egg yolks, lemon extract, half of the lemon zest, and almond meal and beat to incorporate. Gradually add the dry mixture and beat until the dough just holds together. Flatten the dough into a disk, cover with plastic wrap, and refrigerate for 1 hour.

2. Preheat the oven to 325°F and line two baking sheets with parchment paper. Place the dough on a flour-dusted work surface and roll it out to ¼-inch thick. Use cookie cutters to cut the dough into star shapes and place them on the baking sheets.

3. Place the cookies in the oven and bake for about 16 minutes, until set and golden brown. Remove from the oven and let the cookies cool on the baking sheets. Dust with confectioners' sugar and the remaining lemon zest before serving.

A STAR IS BORN

YIELD: 60 COOKIES | ACTIVE TIME: 15 MINUTES | TOTAL TIME: 1 HOUR AND 45 MINUTES

2 sticks unsalted butter, at room temperature

1⅓ cups granulated sugar

1 teaspoon pure vanilla extract

2 large eggs

2 large egg yolks

½ teaspoon cinnamon

1 pinch ground nutmeg

1 cup almond meal

3½ cups all-purpose flour, plus more for dusting

⅔ cup raspberry jam

Confectioners' sugar, for dusting

1. Place the butter, sugar, vanilla, eggs, and egg yolks in a mixing bowl and beat at medium speed with a handheld mixer fitted with the paddle attachment until pale and fluffy, scraping down the sides of the bowl as needed. Add the cinnamon and nutmeg, beat to incorporate, and then add the almond meal and flour. Knead the mixture with your hands until a smooth dough forms. Cover in plastic wrap and refrigerate for 1 hour.

2. Preheat the oven to 350°F and line two baking sheets with parchment paper. Place the dough on a flour-dusted work surface and roll out to ⅛-inch thick. Use cookie cutters to cut the dough into star shapes, and then use a smaller cookie cutter to cut a smaller star shape in the center of half of the cookies. Place the cookies on the baking sheets.

3. Place the cookies in the oven and bake for about 8 minutes, or until lightly browned. Remove from oven and transfer to wire racks to cool completely.

4. Place the raspberry jam in a saucepan and warm over medium-low heat, stirring until smooth. Spread ½ teaspoon of the warm jam on each cookie that was left whole. Place the cookies with the cut-out centers on top, dust with confectioners' sugar, and serve.

PEPPERMINT BARK COOKIES

YIELD: 36 COOKIES | ACTIVE TIME: 45 MINUTES | TOTAL TIME: 2 HOURS AND 30 MINUTES

1½ sticks unsalted
butter, at room
temperature

1 cup granulated sugar

1 large egg, at room
temperature

1 teaspoon pure
vanilla extract

1½ cups all-purpose
flour

¾ cup unsweetened
cocoa powder, plus
more for dusting

1 teaspoon baking
powder

⅛ teaspoon kosher salt

2½ cups white
chocolate chips

1 teaspoon coconut oil

¾ teaspoon pure mint
extract

5 candy canes, crushed

1. Place the butter and sugar in a mixing bowl
   and beat at medium speed with a handheld
   mixer fitted with the paddle attachment until pale and fluffy, scraping down the sides of
   the bowl as needed. Add the egg and vanilla, reduce speed to low, and beat to incorporate.

2. Place the flour, cocoa powder, baking powder, and salt in a mixing bowl and whisk to
   combine. With the handheld mixer running on low speed, gradually add the dry
   mixture to the wet mixture and beat until a
   smooth dough forms. Divide the dough into
   two balls and dust a work surface with cocoa powder. Roll the pieces of dough out to
   ¼-inch thick, place them between pieces of
   parchment paper, and refrigerate for 1 hour.

3. Preheat the oven to 350°F and line two large
   baking sheets with parchment paper. Cut
   the dough into circles and place them on the
   baking sheets.

4. Place in the oven and bake for 10 minutes, until the edges are set and the centers are still soft. Remove from the oven and let the cookies cool on the baking sheets for 5 minutes before transferring them to wire racks to cool completely.

5. Place the white chocolate chips and oil in a microwave-safe bowl and microwave on medium until melted and smooth, removing to stir every 15 seconds. Remove and stir in the mint extract. Working with one cookie at a time, drop it into the white chocolate mixture and turn to coat it all over. Remove the coated cookies and place them on pieces of waxed paper. Sprinkle some of the crushed candy canes on top and let the chocolate set before serving.

29

SNICKERDOODLES

YIELD: 24 COOKIES | ACTIVE TIME: 25 MINUTES | TOTAL TIME: 1 HOUR

3 cups all-purpose
flour

2 teaspoons cream of
tartar

1 teaspoon baking
soda

2½ teaspoons
cinnamon

½ teaspoon kosher salt

2 sticks unsalted
butter, at room
temperature

1⅔ cups granulated
sugar

1 large egg, at room
temperature

2 teaspoons pure
vanilla extract

1. Preheat the oven to 375°F and line two large baking sheets with parchment paper. Whisk together the flour, cream of tartar, baking soda, 1½ teaspoons of the cinnamon, and the salt together in a mixing bowl.

2. Using a handheld mixer fitted with the paddle attachment, cream the butter and 1⅓ cups of the granulated sugar together on medium speed until light and fluffy. Add the egg and vanilla, and beat until combined, scraping down the mixing bowl as needed. With the mixer running on low, add the dry mixture in three increments, waiting until each portion has been incorporated until adding the next. A thick dough will form.

3. Roll tablespoons of the dough into balls. Place the remaining cinnamon and sugar in a mixing bowl and stir to combine. Roll the balls in the mixture until coated and place them on the baking sheets.

4. Bake for 10 minutes, until puffy and very soft. Remove from the oven, press down with a spatula to flatten them out, and let cool on the baking sheets for 10 minutes before transferring to a wire rack to cool completely.

ORANGE SPRITZ

YIELD: 48 COOKIES | ACTIVE TIME:15 MINUTES | TOTAL TIME: 45 MINUTES

2 sticks unsalted butter, at room temperature

1 cup granulated sugar

1 tablespoon light brown sugar

Zest of 1 orange

2 egg yolks

2¼ cups all-purpose flour

¼ teaspoon kosher salt

¼ teaspoon baking soda

Confectioners' sugar, for dusting

1. Preheat oven to 350°F and line two baking sheets with parchment paper. Place the butter, sugars, and orange zest in a mixing bowl and beat at medium speed with a handheld mixer fitted with the paddle attachment until pale and fluffy, scraping down the sides of the bowl as needed. Add the egg yolks and beat to combine. Sift the flour, salt, and baking soda into a separate mixing bowl. Gradually add the dry mixture to the butter mixture and work the mixture with your hands until a smooth dough forms.

2. Shape the dough into small logs, place them in a cookie press, and press desired shapes onto the baking sheets.

3. Place in the oven and bake for 10 to 12 minutes, until the edges start to brown. Remove from the oven and transfer the cookies to wire racks to cool. Dust with confectioners' sugar before serving.

WHITE CHOCOLATE & CRANBERRY COOKIES

YIELD: 48 COOKIES | ACTIVE TIME: 15 MINUTES | TOTAL TIME: 3 HOURS

2¾ cups all-purpose flour

1 teaspoon baking soda

1 teaspoon kosher salt

1 cup unsalted butter, at room temperature

1 cup gently packed light brown sugar

½ cup granulated sugar

2 large eggs, at room temperature

2 teaspoons pure vanilla extract

1½ cups white chocolate chips

1 cup sweetened dried cranberries

1. Place the flour, baking soda, and salt in a large mixing bowl and whisk to combine. Place the butter, brown sugar, and granulated sugar in a separate mixing bowl and beat at medium speed with a handheld mixer fitted with the paddle attachment until pale and fluffy, scraping down the sides of the bowl as needed. Incorporate the eggs one at a time, add the vanilla, and beat to incorporate.

2. With the handheld mixer running on low speed, gradually add the dry mixture to the wet mixture and beat until a smooth dough forms. Add the white chocolate chips and dried cranberries, and fold until evenly distributed. Cover the dough with plastic wrap and refrigerate for 2 hours.

3. Preheat the oven to 350°F and line two large baking sheets with parchment paper. Drop tablespoons of the dough onto the baking sheets and, working with one baking sheet at a time, place them in the oven and bake for about 10 minutes, until lightly browned. Remove from the oven and let cool on the baking sheets for 5 minutes before transferring to wire racks to cool completely.

COCONUT MACAROONS

YIELD: 18 MACAROONS | ACTIVE TIME: 15 MINUTES | TOTAL TIME: 1 HOUR

1 cup unsweetened shredded coconut

2 tablespoons honey

2 tablespoons coconut oil

½ cup all-purpose flour

1 teaspoon pure vanilla extract

¼ teaspoon kosher salt

⅔ cup milk chocolate chips

1. Place all of the ingredients, except for the chocolate chips, in a food processor, and blitz until thoroughly combined.

2. Form tablespoons of the mixture into balls and place them on a parchment-lined baking sheet. Place in the refrigerator for 30 minutes.

3. Place the chocolate chips in a microwave-safe bowl. Microwave on medium until melted and smooth, removing to stir every 15 seconds.

4. Remove the baking sheet from the refrigerator and dip the balls halfway into the melted chocolate. Place them back on the baking sheet, drizzle any remaining chocolate over the top, and place them in the refrigerator until the chocolate is set.

STAINED GLASS COOKIES

YIELD: 24 COOKIES | ACTIVE TIME: 20 MINUTES | TOTAL TIME: 2 HOURS

2 sticks unsalted butter

¾ cup granulated sugar

½ cup gently packed light brown sugar

1 large egg, at room temperature

½ teaspoon pure rum extract

½ teaspoon kosher salt

3¼ cups all-purpose flour, plus more for dusting

½ pound hard candies, crushed

1. Place the butter and sugars in a mixing bowl and beat at medium speed with a handheld mixer fitted with the paddle attachment until light and fluffy. Add the egg, rum extract, and salt, and beat until incorporated. With the mixer running at low speed, gradually add the flour to the mixture and beat until it is a stiff dough. Divide the dough in half and wrap each half in plastic wrap. Flatten each piece of dough and refrigerate for 1 hour.

2. Preheat the oven to 350°F and line two baking sheets with parchment paper. Place the dough on a flour-dusted work surface and roll each piece out to ¼-inch thick. Use cookie cutters to cut the dough into the desired shapes and use smaller cutters to create designs inside of the cookies. Fill the holes with crushed candy and place the cookies on the baking sheets.

3. Place the cookies in the oven and bake for about 10 minutes, until the edges start to brown. Remove the cookies from the oven and let them cool briefly on the baking sheets before transferring them to wire racks to cool completely.

CHOCOLATE TRUFFLES

YIELD: 36 TRUFFLES | ACTIVE TIME: 20 MINUTES | TOTAL TIME: 16 HOURS

1 pound high-quality
bittersweet chocolate

1¼ cups heavy cream

1 pinch kosher salt

½ cup unsweetened
cocoa powder

1. Break the chocolate into small pieces, place it in a food processor, and blitz until it is finely chopped.

2. Place the cream in a saucepan and bring to a simmer over medium heat, stirring frequently. Stir in the salt and chocolate. Remove the pan from heat, cover it, and let sit for 5 minutes. Whisk mixture until smooth and transfer to a square 9-inch baking pan. Let the mixture cool completely, cover with plastic wrap, and refrigerate overnight.

3. Line two baking sheets with parchment paper and place the cocoa powder in a shallow dish. Roll heaping tablespoons of the mixture into balls and roll them in the cocoa powder. Place them on the baking sheets and refrigerate for 30 minutes before serving.

MOM'S SUGAR COOKIES

YIELD: 36 COOKIES | ACTIVE TIME: 15 MINUTES | TOTAL TIME: 1 HOUR AND 45 MINUTES

¾ cup shortening

4 tablespoons unsalted butter, at room temperature

1 cup granulated sugar

2 eggs

½ teaspoon pure lemon extract

½ teaspoon pure vanilla extract

2⅔ cups all-purpose flour, sifted, plus more for dusting

1 teaspoon baking powder

½ teaspoon kosher salt

Colored sugars, for decoration

1. Place the shortening, butter, and sugar in a mixing bowl and beat at medium speed with a handheld mixer fitted with the paddle attachment until pale and fluffy, scraping down the sides of the bowl as needed. Add the eggs and extracts, and beat to incorporate. Place the flour, baking powder, and salt in a separate bowl and stir to combine. With the handheld mixer running on low speed, gradually add the dry mixture to the wet mixture and beat until a smooth dough forms. Cover the dough with plastic wrap and refrigerate for 1 hour.

2. Preheat the oven to 350°F and line two large baking sheets with parchment paper. Place the dough on a flour-dusted work surface and roll out to ⅛-inch thick. Use cookie cutters to cut the dough into desired shapes and place them on the baking sheets.

3. Place the cookies in the oven and bake for 6 to 8 minutes, until slightly brown. Remove the cookies from the oven and transfer to a wire rack to cool. Sprinkle with colored sugars, if desired.

CHOCOLATE CRINKLE COOKIES

YIELD: 72 COOKIES | ACTIVE TIME: 15 MINUTES | TOTAL TIME: 5 HOURS

1⅓ cups unsweetened cocoa powder

2½ cups granulated sugar

½ cup vegetable oil

4 eggs

2 teaspoons pure vanilla extract

2¼ cups all-purpose flour

2 teaspoons baking powder

½ teaspoon kosher salt

½ cup confectioners' sugar

1. Place the cocoa powder, granulated sugar, and vegetable oil in a mixing bowl and stir to combine. Incorporate the eggs one at a time and then stir in the vanilla. Place the flour, baking powder, and salt in a separate bowl and stir to combine. Stir the dry mixture into the wet mixture and work the mixture with your hands until a soft dough forms. Cover the dough with plastic wrap and refrigerate for 4 hours.

2. Preheat the oven to 350°F and line two baking sheets with parchment paper. Place the confectioners' sugar in a shallow dish. Form tablespoons of the dough into balls. Roll the balls in the confectioners' sugar until coated and place them on the baking sheets.

3. Place in the oven and bake for 8 to 10 minutes, until the edges are firm. Remove from the oven and let the cookies cool for 1 minute on the baking sheets before transferring to wire racks to cool completely.

BOURBON BALLS

YIELD: 24 COOKIES | ACTIVE TIME: 15 MINUTES | TOTAL TIME: 3 HOURS

2 sticks unsalted butter, at room temperature

8 cups confectioners' sugar, plus more for sprinkling

½ cup bourbon

½ teaspoon kosher salt

Melted chocolate, for topping

Unsweetened cocoa powder, for topping

Shredded coconut, for topping

1. Place the butter and half of the confectioners' sugar in a mixing bowl and beat at medium speed with a handheld mixer fitted with the paddle attachment until pale and fluffy, scraping down the sides of the bowl as needed. Add the remaining sugar, bourbon, and salt, and beat until incorporated. Refrigerate for 2 hours.

2. Line baking sheets with parchment paper. Form tablespoons of the mixture into balls. Coat the balls in melted chocolate, cocoa powder, confectioners' sugar, and/or shredded coconut and then transfer the sheets to the refrigerator. Chill for 45 minutes before serving.

GRASSHOPPER COOKIES

For the Cookies

2 sticks unsalted butter

¼ cup granulated sugar

1 large egg yolk, at
room temperature

½ teaspoon pure
vanilla extract

½ teaspoon baking
powder

½ teaspoon kosher salt

½ cup unsweetened
cocoa powder

2 cups all-purpose
flour

½ cup semisweet
chocolate chips, melted

For the Filling

½ cup heavy cream

1½ tablespoons light
corn syrup

2 cups white chocolate
chips

2 tablespoons unsalted
butter

1 teaspoon pure mint
extract

¼ teaspoon red or
green food coloring
(optional)

1. To begin preparations for the cookies, place the butter and sugar in a mixing bowl and beat at medium speed with a handheld mixer fitted with the paddle attachment. Beat in the egg yolk, vanilla, baking powder, and salt, and then slowly incorporate the cocoa powder and flour until a stiff dough forms.

2. Place the dough on a sheet of waxed paper and roll it into a log that is 2½ inches in diameter. Cover in plastic wrap and refrigerate for 2 hours.

3. To prepare the filling, place the cream and corn syrup in a small saucepan and bring to a simmer. Stir in the white chocolate chips, butter, and mint extract. Cover the pan, and remove from heat. Allow mixture to sit for 5 minutes. Stir well and, if using, stir in food coloring.

4. Preheat the oven to 350°F, line two baking sheets with parchment paper, and cut the chilled dough into ½-inch-thick slices. Place the cookies on the baking sheets, place them in the oven, and bake until the edges start to brown, about 10 minutes. Remove from

the oven and let cool on the baking sheets for 2 minutes before transferring to wire racks to cool completely.

5. When the cookies are cool, dip them in the melted chocolate until completely coated. Place the cookies back on the baking sheet and place it in the refrigerator until the chocolate has hardened, about 20 minutes. Beat the filling with a handheld mixer on medium speed until it is light and fluffy. Place a dollop on the flat side of 1 cookie and top with the flat side of another cookie. Repeat until all of the cookies have been used.

PB & J THUMBPRINTS

YIELD: 24 COOKIES | ACTIVE TIME: 20 MINUTES | TOTAL TIME: 1 HOUR

¾ cup firmly packed light brown sugar

1 stick unsalted butter, at room temperature

1 cup creamy peanut butter

1 large egg, at room temperature

½ teaspoon pure vanilla extract

1 teaspoon baking soda

⅛ teaspoon kosher salt

1 cup all-purpose flour

1½ cups seedless raspberry jam

1. Preheat the oven to 375°F and line two baking sheets with parchment paper. Place the brown sugar, butter, and peanut butter in a mixing bowl and beat at medium speed with a handheld mixer fitted with the paddle attachment until light and fluffy. Add the egg, vanilla, baking soda, and salt and beat for 1 minute. With the mixer running on low, add the flour and beat until a soft dough forms.

2. Form tablespoons of the dough into balls and place them on the baking sheets. Use your index finger to make a large depression in the center of each ball. Place the cookies into the oven and bake for 10 to 12 minutes, until the edges are brown. Remove the cookies from the oven and let cool for 2 minutes on the baking sheets before transferring them to wire racks to cool completely.

3. While the cookies are cooling, place the raspberry jam in a saucepan and warm over medium heat. Bring to a boil, while stirring frequently, and cook until the jam has been reduced by one-quarter. Spoon a teaspoon of the jam into each cookie and let it set before serving.

THE NIGHT BEFORE CHRISTMAS

Tradition dictates that a plate of
cookies must be left out for Santa to
reward him for all his hard work.
The cookies in this chapter are sure
to keep him going (and go great with
a cup of coffee).

ALMOND MERINGUES WITH CREAM FILLING

YIELD: 24 COOKIES | ACTIVE TIME: 30 MINUTES | TOTAL TIME: 2 HOURS

**Almond Meringues
(see page 109)**

⅔ cup chocolate chips

**2 teaspoons instant
espresso powder**

**1 tablespoon unsalted
butter, at room
temperature**

**½ teaspoon pure
vanilla extract**

**1¼ cups confectioners'
sugar, plus more for
dusting**

1. When the Almond Meringues are almost cool, place the chocolate chips in a microwave-safe bowl and microwave on medium until melted and smooth, removing to stir every 15 seconds. Add the espresso powder and butter and stir to combine. Add the vanilla and confectioners' sugar and beat at high speed with a handheld mixer fitted with the paddle attachment until soft peaks form.

2. Place a dollop of cream on the bottom of one of the meringues. Top with another meringue, dust with additional confectioners' sugar, and serve.

CHRISTMAS ORNAMENT COOKIES

YIELD: 24 COOKIES | ACTIVE TIME: 25 MINUTES | TOTAL TIME: 1 HOUR AND 30 MINUTES

2¼ cups
all-purpose flour, plus
more for dusting

½ cup granulated
sugar

1 pinch kosher salt

1 egg

14 tablespoons
unsalted butter

1¾ cups confectioners'
sugar, plus more for
dusting

½ cup white fondant

½ cup blue fondant

½ cup
green fondant

Juice of 1 lemon

Food coloring, for
decoration

Caster sugar, for
sprinkling

1. Place the flour, granulated sugar, and salt in a mixing bowl and stir to combine. Make a well in the center. Beat together the egg and butter, and pour the mixture into the well. Knead the mixture with your hands until a smooth dough forms. Shape the dough into a ball, cover with plastic wrap, and refrigerate for 30 minutes.

2. Preheat the oven to 350°F and line two baking sheets with parchment paper. Place the dough on a flour-dusted work surface and roll out into a ¼-inch-thick square. Use cookie cutters to cut the dough into Christmas ornament shapes and place them on the baking sheets.

3. Place the cookies in the oven and bake for about 12 minutes, until a light golden brown. Remove from the oven and let the cookies cool on the baking sheets for a few minutes before transferring them to wire racks to cool completely.

4. Dust a work surface with confectioners' sugar and roll out the fondant until it is ¼-inch thick. Cut the fondant into shapes that will fit the cookies. Brush the shaped fondant lightly with water and affix to the cookies.

5. Place the confectioners' sugar and lemon juice in a bowl and stir until the frosting has the desired consistency. If using multiple shades of food coloring, divide the frosting between several small bowls and incorporate the food coloring. Place the frosting in a piping bag fitted with a fine tip and decorate cookies as desired. Sprinkle caster sugar on top and let the frosting set before serving.

SHORTBREAD SNOWFLAKES

YIELD: 12 COOKIES | ACTIVE TIME: 30 MINUTES | TOTAL TIME: 2 HOURS

2¼ cups all-purpose flour, plus more for dusting

6 tablespoons cornstarch

18 tablespoons unsalted butter, divided into tablespoons

1⅔ cups confectioners' sugar

½ teaspoon kosher salt

Boiling water, as needed

Edible silver balls, for decoration

1. Place the flour, cornstarch, butter, ⅔ cup of the sugar, and the salt in a food processor and pulse until the dough starts to hold together. Knead the dough until it is a ball, cover in plastic wrap, and refrigerate for 1 hour.

2. Preheat the oven to 350°F and line two baking sheets with parchment paper. Place the dough on a flour-dusted work surface and roll it out to ¼-inch thick. Use cookie cutters to cut the dough into snowflake shapes and place them on the baking sheets.

3. Place the cookies in the oven and bake for about 12 minutes, until golden brown. Remove from the oven and let the cookies cool on the baking sheets for a few minutes before transferring to a wire rack to cool completely.

4. Place the remaining confectioners' sugar in a mixing bowl and incorporate boiling water until the frosting achieves the desired consistency. Spread the frosting over half of the cookies and affix some of the silver balls. Dot the edges and centers of the undecorated cookies with frosting and affix silver balls to each dot. Let the frosting and balls set before serving.

ORANGE SPICE COOKIES

1 cup granulated sugar

Zest of 1 orange

2¼ cups all-purpose flour

1 teaspoon baking soda

1½ teaspoons cinnamon

1½ teaspoons ground ginger

½ teaspoon ground cloves

¼ teaspoon ground allspice

¼ teaspoon black pepper

¼ teaspoon kosher salt

1½ sticks unsalted butter, at room temperature

⅓ cup firmly packed dark brown sugar

1 large egg yolk

1 teaspoon pure vanilla extract

½ cup molasses

1. Preheat the oven to 375°F and line two baking sheets with parchment paper. Place ⅔ cup of the granulated sugar and 2 teaspoons of orange zest in a food processor and pulse until combined. Place the sugar mixture in a square baking dish and set aside. Place the flour, baking soda, spices, and salt in mixing bowl, whisk to combine, and set aside.

2. Place the butter, remaining orange zest, brown sugar, and remaining granulated sugar in a mixing bowl and beat at medium speed with a handheld mixer fitted with the paddle attachment until pale and fluffy, scraping down the sides of the bowl as needed. Add the egg yolk and vanilla, reduce speed to low, and beat to incorporate. Add the molasses and beat to incorporate. Add the dry mixture and beat until the dough just holds together.

3. Form tablespoons of the dough into balls, roll them in the orange sugar, and place them on the baking sheets. Working with one sheet of cookies at a time, place them in the oven and bake for about 10 minutes, until they are set at the edges but the centers are still soft. Remove from the oven and let cool on the baking sheets for 5 minutes before transferring them to wire racks to cool completely.

TANNENBAUM COOKIES

YIELD: 40 COOKIES | ACTIVE TIME: 20 MINUTES | TOTAL TIME: 1 HOUR AND 30 MINUTES

1½ sticks unsalted butter

½ cup brown sugar, plus more as needed

1 egg, lightly beaten

1 teaspoon pure vanilla extract

1 pinch kosher salt

½ cup almond meal

2 teaspoons ground allspice

All-purpose flour, for dusting

2½ tablespoons minced hazelnuts

Brown sugar, as needed

1 cup confectioners' sugar

Juice of 1 lemon

2 to 3 tablespoons pine nuts

1. Place the butter and brown sugar in a mixing bowl and beat at medium speed with a handheld mixer fitted with the paddle attachment until pale and fluffy, scraping down the bowl as needed. Add the egg and vanilla, reduce speed to low, and beat to incorporate. Stir in the salt, almond meal, and allspice. Knead the mixture with your hands until a smooth dough forms, shape the dough into a ball, cover in plastic wrap, and refrigerate for 30 minutes.

2. Preheat the oven to 350°F and line two large baking sheets with parchment paper. Place the dough on a flour-dusted work surface and roll it out to ¼-inch thick. Use cookie cutters to cut the dough into Christmas tree shapes and place them on the baking sheets. Sprinkle the hazelnuts over one-third of the cookies, leaving two-thirds undecorated.

3. Place the cookies in the oven and bake for about 10 minutes, until the edges are browned. Remove cookies from oven and sprinkle one-third of the remaining undecorated cookies with additional brown sugar. Transfer the cookies to wire racks to cool completely.

4. Place the confectioners' sugar and lemon juice in a mixing bowl and stir until the frosting achieves the desired consistency. Cover the remaining undecorated cookies with the frosting and decorate these with the pine nuts. Let the frosting set before serving.

WALNUT COOKIES WITH CHOCOLATE FILLING

YIELD: 24 COOKIES | ACTIVE TIME: 30 MINUTES | TOTAL TIME: 2 HOURS

For the Cookies

1 stick unsalted butter, at room temperature

⅓ cup firmly packed brown sugar

¼ teaspoon kosher salt

½ teaspoon cinnamon

1 pinch ground ginger

1 teaspoon pure vanilla extract

1 tablespoon walnut liqueur (such as Nocello)

1 cup all-purpose flour

2 tablespoons cornstarch

½ cup minced walnuts

For the Filling

9 tablespoons heavy whipping cream

1 tablespoon light corn syrup

1 cup bittersweet chocolate chips

½ cup minced walnuts

1. To begin preparations for the cookies, place the butter, brown sugar, salt, cinnamon, ginger, vanilla, and walnut liqueur in a mixing bowl and beat until pale and fluffy, scraping down the sides of the bowl as needed. Add the flour, cornstarch, and walnuts and beat until a smooth dough forms. Cover in plastic wrap and refrigerate for 30 minutes.

2. Preheat the oven to 375°F and line two baking sheets with parchment paper. Form the dough into balls and place them on the baking sheets. Place in the oven and bake for 10 to 12 minutes, until the edges are golden brown. Remove and let cool for 5 minutes on the baking sheets before transferring to wire racks to cool completely.

3. To prepare the filling, warm the cream and corn syrup over medium heat until the mixture starts to steam. Remove the pan from heat, add the chocolate chips, and stir until they have melted. Continue stirring until the mixture has cooled.

4. Spread the cooled filling on the flat side of each cookie, sandwich the cookies together, and roll the edges of the filling in the walnuts.

HERE COMES SANTA CLAUS

YIELD: 24 COOKIES | ACTIVE TIME: 20 MINUTES | TOTAL TIME: 16 HOURS

⅓ cup honey

⅓ cup granulated sugar

4 tablespoons unsalted butter

1¾ cups all-purpose flour, plus more for dusting

2 teaspoons ground ginger

2 teaspoons cinnamon

½ teaspoon ground anise

½ teaspoon ground cloves

¼ teaspoon potash

¼ teaspoon hartshorn salt

¼ cup chopped candied orange peels

1 tablespoon water

2 tablespoons fresh lemon juice

2¼ cups confectioners' sugar

Red food coloring, as needed

1. Place the honey, sugar, and butter in a saucepan and cook over medium heat, stirring until the sugar dissolves. Remove from heat and let cool. Place the flour and the spices in a mixing bowl and stir to combine. Stir the potash and the hartshorn salt into the honey mixture. Stir in the flour mixture and the candied orange peels, cover the dough with plastic wrap, and refrigerate overnight.

2. Preheat the oven to 400°F and line two or three baking sheets with parchment paper. Place the dough on a flour-dusted work surface and roll it out to ¼-inch thick. Cut the dough into triangles and place them on the baking sheets. Place the cookies in the oven and bake for about 20 minutes, until golden brown. Remove from the oven and let the cookies cool on the baking sheets.

3. Place the water, lemon juice, and confectioners' sugar in a mixing bowl and stir until smooth. Place 6 tablespoons of the frosting in a separate bowl, add the red food coloring, and stir to incorporate. Decorate the cookies, using the red frosting for the hats. Let the frosting set before serving.

CHOCOLATE TURTLE COOKIES

YIELD: 24 COOKIES | ACTIVE TIME: 20 MINUTES | TOTAL TIME: 2 HOURS

1 cup all-purpose flour

⅔ cup unsweetened cocoa powder

1 pinch kosher salt

1 stick unsalted butter, at room temperature

14 tablespoons granulated sugar

1 egg yolk

2 tablespoons milk

1 teaspoon pure vanilla extract

1 egg white

1 cup minced pecans

14 soft caramel candies

3 tablespoons heavy cream

1. Place the flour, cocoa powder, and salt in a mixing bowl and stir to combine. Place the butter and sugar in a mixing bowl and beat at medium speed with a handheld mixer fitted with the paddle attachment until pale and fluffy, scraping down the sides of the bowl as needed. Add the egg yolk, milk, and vanilla and beat until incorporated. With the handheld mixer running on low speed, gradually add the dry mixture to the wet mixture and beat until a smooth dough forms. Shape the dough into a ball, cover it with plastic wrap, and then flatten into a disk. Refrigerate the dough for 1 hour.

2. Preheat the oven to 350°F and line two large baking sheets with parchment paper. Place the egg white in a bowl and whisk until frothy. Place the pecans in a shallow dish. Form tablespoons of the dough into balls, dip the balls in the egg white, and roll in the pecans. Place the balls on the baking sheets.

3. Place the cookies in the oven and bake, rotating the sheets halfway through, for about 12 minutes, until set. Remove from the oven

and use the measuring spoon to make an indentation in the center of the cookies. Let the cookies cool on the baking sheets for 5 minutes before transferring to wire racks to cool completely.

4. Place the caramels and heavy cream in a microwave-safe bowl and microwave on medium until the caramels are melted and the mixture is smooth, removing to stir every 15 seconds. Remove from the microwave and allow the mixture to cool slightly. Fill each cookie with ½ teaspoon of the mixture and let it cool completely before serving.

ICY MOLASSES DROPS

YIELD: 24 COOKIES | ACTIVE TIME: 40 MINUTES | TOTAL TIME: 2 HOURS

3 tablespoons currants

Zest of 3 oranges

3 tablespoons raisins

2 teaspoons brandy

7 tablespoons unsalted butter

⅓ cup gently packed light brown sugar

½ teaspoon pure vanilla extract

2 teaspoons molasses

1 teaspoon pumpkin pie spice

¼ cup sliced almonds, chopped

1⅓ cups self-rising flour

¼ cup almond meal

1 cup demerara sugar

1¾ cups confectioners' sugar

1 tablespoon fresh lemon juice

Hot water (125°F), as needed

4 candied cherries, minced, for decoration

Mint leaves, for decoration

1. Place the currants, 1 tablespoon of the orange zest, raisins, and brandy in a bowl, stir to combine, and cover with plastic wrap. Let stand for 1 hour.

2. Place the mixture in a food processor and puree until smooth. Preheat the oven to 350°F and line two large baking sheets with parchment paper. Place the butter and brown sugar in a mixing bowl and beat at medium speed with a handheld mixer fitted with the paddle attachment until pale and fluffy, scraping down the sides of the bowl as needed. Add the remaining zest and vanilla, reduce speed to low, and beat to incorporate.

3. Place the molasses in a saucepan and gently warm over medium heat. Add to the butter mixture, stir to combine, and then incorporate the pumpkin pie spice. Add the chopped almonds, flour, almond meal, and chopped fruit and stir until a smooth dough forms.

4. Place the demerara sugar in a shallow dish. Form tablespoons of the dough into balls, roll them in the sugar, and place them on the baking sheets. Place the cookies in the

oven and bake for 10 minutes, until the cookies look dry and slightly cracked on the surface. Remove from the oven and let cool on the baking sheets for 5 minutes before transferring to wire racks to cool completely.

5. Sift the confectioners' sugar into a deep bowl, add the lemon juice, and beat until combined. Incorporate tablespoons of hot water until the frosting achieves the desired consistency. Spoon some of the frosting over each cookie, allowing it to run down the sides a little. Decorate each cookie with a piece of candied cherry and a mint leaf. Let set before serving.

KIDS' FAVORITES

Delicious, decorative, and fun to make, these cookies are perfect for getting the kids excited about carrying on holiday traditions.

PEANUT BUTTER PRANCERS

YIELD: 48 COOKIES | ACTIVE TIME: 10 MINUTES | TOTAL TIME: 1 HOUR

1 stick unsalted butter, at room temperature

¾ cup creamy peanut butter

⅓ cup granulated sugar

3½ tablespoons light brown sugar

1 large egg

1 teaspoon pure vanilla extract

1⅔ cups all-purpose flour

1 teaspoon baking soda

½ teaspoon kosher salt

48 red M&M's

96 miniature semisweet chocolate chips

96 miniature pretzel centers

1. Preheat the oven to 350°F and line two or three baking sheets with parchment paper. Place the butter, peanut butter, granulated sugar, and brown sugar in a mixing bowl and beat at medium speed with a handheld mixer fitted with the paddle attachment until pale and fluffy, scraping down the sides of the bowl as needed. Add the egg and vanilla and beat to incorporate. Gradually add the flour, baking soda, and salt, reduce speed to low, and beat until a smooth dough forms.

2. Roll tablespoons of the dough into balls and place them on the baking sheets. Place the cookies in the oven and bake for about 8 minutes, until the cookies are just set. Remove from the oven and place an M&M for a nose, two chocolate chips for eyes, and two pretzel centers for antlers on each cookie. Carefully transfer the cookies to wire racks to cool completely.

CHOCOLATE-COVERED MARSHMALLOW COOKIES

YIELD: 24 COOKIES | ACTIVE TIME: 30 MINUTES | TOTAL TIME: 3 HOURS AND 30 MINUTES

2⅔ cups all-purpose flour, plus more for dusting

⅔ cup sugar

½ teaspoon kosher salt

¾ teaspoon baking powder

½ teaspoon baking soda

1 teaspoon cinnamon

1½ sticks unsalted butter, divided into tablespoons

3 large eggs, lightly beaten

12 large marshmallows, halved

2 cups dark chocolate chips

1 tablespoon coconut oil

1. Place the flour, sugar, salt, baking powder, baking soda, and cinnamon in a mixing bowl and whisk to combine. Add the butter and work the mixture with a pastry blender until it is coarse crumbs. Add the eggs and stir until a stiff dough forms. Shape the dough into a ball, cover with plastic wrap, and refrigerate for 1 hour.

2. Preheat the oven to 375°F and line two baking sheets with parchment paper. Place the dough on a flour-dusted work surface and roll out to ¼-inch thick. Cut the dough into 24 rounds and place them on the baking sheets.

3. Place in the oven and bake for about 10 minutes, until the edges have browned. Remove from the oven and transfer the cookies to wire racks to cool completely. Leave the oven on.

4. When the cookies are cool, place a marshmallow half on each cookie. Place them back in the oven and, while keeping a close eye on the cookies, bake until the marshmallows collapse. Remove from oven and let cool completely on the baking sheets.

5. Place the chocolate chips in a microwave-safe bowl and microwave on medium until melted and smooth, removing to stir every 15 seconds. Add the coconut oil to the melted chocolate and stir until incorporated. Drop the cookies into the chocolate, turning to coat all sides. Carefully remove the coated cookies with a fork, hold them over the bowl to let any excess chocolate drip off, and place on pieces of parchment paper. Let the chocolate set before serving.

GRAHAM CRACKER BARS

YIELD: 54 BARS | ACTIVE TIME: 20 MINUTES | TOTAL TIME: 1 HOUR AND 30 MINUTES

For the Bars

1 stick unsalted butter, melted, plus more for greasing pan

3⅓ cups graham cracker crumbs

2 cups chopped almonds

⅔ cup granulated sugar

2 cups shredded unsweetened coconut

1 (14 oz.) can sweetened condensed milk

For the Topping

1⅓ cups firmly packed light brown sugar

6 tablespoons heavy whipping cream

4 tablespoons unsalted butter, chopped

¾ cup semisweet chocolate chips

1. Preheat the oven to 350°F and lightly grease a 9 x 13-inch baking pan with some of the butter. To begin preparations for the bars, place the graham cracker crumbs, ¾ cup of the chopped almonds, sugar, and butter in a food processor and blitz until the mixture is coarse crumbs. Press the mixture into the baking pan, place in the oven, and bake for 8 to 10 minutes, until lightly browned. Remove from the oven and let cool.

2. Place the coconut and milk in a bowl, and stir to combine. Spread the mixture over the warm crust. Sprinkle the remaining almonds on top, return the pan to the oven, and bake for 12 minutes, until the edges are lightly browned. Remove from the oven and let cool in the pan.

3. To prepare the topping, place the brown sugar, cream, and butter in a saucepan and bring to a boil, stirring constantly. Boil for 1 minute, remove from heat, and add the chocolate chips. Stir until melted, spread the mixture over the bars in an even layer, and let them cool before cutting.

CINNAMON STARS

YIELD: 24 COOKIES | ACTIVE TIME: 10 MINUTES | TOTAL TIME: 1 HOUR

2 cups confectioners' sugar, plus more for dusting

5 cups sliced almonds

1½ teaspoons cinnamon

3 large egg whites, at room temperature

1 pinch kosher salt

1 tablespoon raspberry or black currant jam

12 maraschino cherries, halved

1. Place ½ cup of the confectioners' sugar, the almonds, and cinnamon in a food processor and blitz until the almonds are finely ground.

2. Place the egg whites and salt in a mixing bowl and beat at low speed with a handheld mixer fitted with the whisk attachment until soft peaks form. With the mixer running, slowly add the remaining confectioners' sugar and beat until stiff peaks form. Set about ⅔ cup of the meringue aside. Add the almond mixture and the jam to the remaining meringue and fold until the meringue is a stiff dough.

3. Preheat the oven to 250°F and line two baking sheets with parchment paper. Place the dough on a sheet of parchment paper that has been dusted with confectioners' sugar. Flatten the dough, place another piece of parchment on top, and roll it out to ¼-inch thick. Use a cookie cutter to cut the dough into star shapes and place them on the baking sheets. Pat the cherry halves dry with paper towels and place one in the center of each cookie.

4. Bake for about 25 minutes, until the bottoms are a light golden brown and the meringue is set. Turn off the oven, open the oven door, and allow cookies to dry out in the oven for 15 minutes before serving.

REINDEER COOKIES

YIELD: 36 COOKIES | ACTIVE TIME: 20 MINUTES | TOTAL TIME: 3 HOURS

2¾ cups all-purpose flour, plus more for dusting

2 cups almond meal

2 tablespoons unsweetened cocoa powder

1 teaspoon cinnamon

2 cups confectioners' sugar

1 pinch kosher salt

3 sticks unsalted butter, chilled and chopped

1 egg

2 egg yolks

2 cups chocolate chips

2 teaspoons fresh lemon juice

1. Place the flour, almond meal, cocoa powder, cinnamon, 1¼ cups of the confectioners' sugar, and the salt in a mixing bowl and stir to combine. Form a well in the center and distribute the butter around the well. Place the egg and the egg yolks in the well and work the mixture with a pastry blender until it is coarse crumbs. Knead the mixture with your hands until it is a smooth dough. Shape the dough into a ball, cover with plastic wrap, and refrigerate for 2 hours.

2. Preheat the oven to 375°F and line two baking sheets with parchment paper. Place the dough on a flour-dusted work surface and roll it out into a ⅛-inch-thick square. Using a properly sized cookie cutter, cut out 72 reindeer, and place them on the baking sheets.

3. Bake for about 6 minutes, until the edges start to brown. Remove from the oven and transfer to wire racks to cool.

4. Place the chocolate chips in a micro-wave-safe bowl and microwave on medium until melted and smooth, removing to stir every 15 seconds. Spread the melted choco-

late on half of the cookies, taking care not to spread any chocolate on the legs of the reindeer. Place the remaining cookies on top to form sandwiches.

5. Place the lemon juice and the remaining confectioners' sugar in a mixing bowl and stir until the frosting achieves the desired consistency. Place the frosting in a piping bag fitted with a fine tip and pipe markings and eyes on the reindeer. Let the frosting set before serving.

MITTEN SUGAR COOKIES

YIELD: 24 COOKIES | ACTIVE TIME: 1 HOUR | TOTAL TIME: 2 HOURS AND 30 MINUTES

3¼ cups
all-purpose flour,
sifted

1 teaspoon baking
powder

½ teaspoon kosher salt

2 sticks
unsalted butter, at
room temperature

2⅔ cups
granulated sugar

2 large eggs

2 teaspoons pure
vanilla extract

3½ cups confectioners'
sugar, sifted

2 tablespoons
meringue powder

4½ tablespoons water

Red food coloring, for
decoration

Red decorative sugar,
for decoration

White decorative
sugar, for decoration

1. Sift the flour, baking powder, and salt into a mixing bowl. Place the butter and granulated sugar in a separate mixing bowl, and beat at medium speed with a handheld mixer fitted with the paddle attachment until pale and fluffy, scraping down the sides of the bowl as needed. Add the eggs and vanilla, reduce speed to low, and beat to incorporate. Gradually add the dry mixture and beat until the dough just holds together. Divide the dough into quarters, flatten each piece into a disk, cover with plastic wrap, and refrigerate for 1 hour.

2. Preheat the oven to 325°F and line a baking sheet with parchment paper. Remove one disk of dough from the refrigerator and let stand at room temperature for 10 minutes. Roll out the dough between two pieces of parchment paper until it is ¼-inch thick. Use cookie cutters to cut the dough into mitten shapes and place them on the baking sheet. Place the baking sheet in the freezer and freeze for 15 minutes.

3. Remove the baking sheet from the freezer and place it in the oven. Bake, rotating the sheet halfway through, for about 16 minutes,

until the edges are almost browned. Remove from the oven and let the cookies cool on the baking sheets for a few minutes before transferring them to wire racks to cool completely. Repeat with the remaining pieces of dough.

4. Place the confectioners' sugar and meringue powder in a mixing bowl and beat at low speed with a handheld mixer fitted with the paddle attachment. Beat until the frosting has lost its sheen, about 7 minutes. Add the water a little bit at a time, making sure each addition has been incorporated before adding the next portion. Divide the frosting between two bowls, add the red food coloring to one, and stir to incorporate. Place each bowl of frosting in a separate piping bag and pipe the red frosting all over the surface of each cookie, leaving about ½ inch on the bottom of the cookie uncovered. Cover the bottom portion with the white frosting and let the frostings set.

5. When the frostings have set, sprinkle the decorative sugars on top of their respective colors. Make decorative snowflakes with any remaining white frosting and let set before serving.

SWEETHEARTS

YIELD: 20 COOKIES | ACTIVE TIME: 45 MINUTES | TOTAL TIME: 1 HOUR AND 30 MINUTES

10 tablespoons unsalted butter

¾ cup granulated sugar

2 egg yolks

1¾ cups all-purpose flour, plus more for dusting

1 cup hard candies, lightly crushed

2¼ cups confectioners' sugar

Juice of 1 lemon

1 egg white, lightly beaten

Pink food coloring, as needed

Edible baubles, for decoration

1. Place the butter and granulated sugar in a mixing bowl and beat at medium speed with a handheld mixer fitted with the paddle attachment until pale and fluffy, scraping down the bowl as needed. Add the egg yolks and beat to incorporate. Add the flour and knead the dough with your hands until a dough forms. Shape the dough into a ball, cover with plastic wrap, and refrigerate for 30 minutes.

2. Preheat the oven to 350°F and line two large baking sheets with parchment paper. Place the dough on a flour-dusted work surface and roll it out to ¼-inch thick. Use cookie cutters to cut the dough into heart shapes. Use a smaller cookie cutter to cut a heart in the center of each cookie. Place the cookies on the baking sheets. Fill the smaller hearts with the hard candies.

3. Bake for about 10 minutes, until the edges are browned and the candies have melted. Remove cookies from oven and let cool on the baking sheets.

4. Place the confectioners' sugar, lemon juice, and egg white in a mixing bowl and stir until the frosting achieves the desired consistency. Place some of the frosting in a separate bowl, add the pink food coloring, and stir to incorporate. Place each color of frosting in a separate piping bag and frost the edges of the cookies. Affix the edible baubles to the frosting and let them set before serving.

ICY TREE POPS

YIELD: 12 COOKIES | ACTIVE TIME: 30 MINUTES | TOTAL TIME: 1 HOUR AND 30 MINUTES

12 lollipop sticks

10 tablespoons unsalted butter

½ cup light brown sugar

3 tablespoons light corn syrup or honey

2⅓ cups all-purpose flour, plus more for dusting

1 teaspoon baking soda

1 teaspoon ground ginger

1 teaspoon cinnamon

1 pinch kosher salt

1 cup confectioners' sugar

1 tablespoon hot water (125°F)

Christmas-colored M&M's, for decoration

1. Place the lollipop sticks in a bowl of cold water. Preheat the oven to 400°F and line two baking sheets with parchment paper. Place the butter, brown sugar, and corn syrup or honey in a saucepan. Cook, while stirring, over medium heat until the sugar has dissolved and the butter has melted. Remove from heat and let the mixture cool slightly.

2. Sift the flour, baking soda, spices, and salt into a mixing bowl, stir in the butter mixture, and stir until a stiff dough forms. Let stand for 5 minutes.

3. Place the dough on a flour-dusted work surface and roll out to ¼-inch thick. Use cookie cutters to cut dough into Christmas tree shapes and place them on the baking sheets. Press the soaked lollipop sticks into the cookies about one-third of the way up.

4. Bake for about 10 minutes, until the edges have browned. Remove from the oven and let cool on the baking sheets for 10 minutes before transferring them to wire racks to cool completely.

5. Place the confectioners' sugar and the hot water in a mixing bowl and stir until the icing achieves the desired consistency. Spread the icing over the cookies and decorate with the M&M's.

91

GINGERBREAD REINDEER

YIELD: 12 COOKIES | ACTIVE TIME: 30 MINUTES | TOTAL TIME: 16 HOURS

10 tablespoons
unsalted butter,
divided into
tablespoons

¾ cup honey

1½ cups gently packed
light brown sugar

1 cup almond
meal

2¾ cups all-purpose
flour, plus more for
dusting

½ teaspoon baking
soda

1 teaspoon cinnamon

2 teaspoons
Gingerbread Spice
(see page 94)

Zest of 1 lemon

1 large egg

1¾ cups confectioners'
sugar

3 tablespoons fresh
lemon juice

Candy eyeballs, for
decoration

Red sugar pearls, for
decoration

1. Place the butter, honey, and brown sugar in a saucepan and warm over medium heat, stirring until the sugar dissolves. Transfer to a large mixing bowl and let cool for 5 minutes.

2. Add the almond meal, flour, baking soda, spices, lemon zest, and egg, and work the mixture with your hands until a smooth dough forms. Place the dough on a flour-dusted work surface and flatten it into a disk. Cover in plastic wrap and refrigerate overnight.

3. Preheat the oven to 400°F and line two baking sheets with parchment paper. Place the dough on a flour-dusted work surface and roll it out to ¼-inch thick. Cut the dough into large (3 inches in diameter) and small (1½ inches in diameter) circles. Form the remaining dough into small pretzel shapes. Place on the baking sheets, place in the oven, and bake for about 15 minutes, until set and golden brown. It may be necessary to remove the pretzels earlier. Remove from oven and transfer the pieces to a wire rack to cool completely.

4. Place the confectioners' sugar and lemon juice in a mixing bowl, and stir until the

frosting achieves the desired consistency. Use the frosting to affix the pretzels to the large circles as antlers. Affix the small circles onto the larger ones as noses. Decorate with the candy eyeballs and red sugar pearls. Let set before serving.

GINGERBREAD SPICE

YIELD: ABOUT 5 CUPS
ACTIVE TIME: 5 MINUTES
TOTAL TIME: 5 MINUTES

¾ cup cinnamon

½ cup ground cloves

⅓ cup ground nutmeg

½ cup ground ginger

1 cup ground fennel

1 cup coriander

1 cup ground anise

1. Place all of the ingredients in a large mixing bowl and stir until thoroughly combined. Store in an airtight container for up to 6 months.

SNOWMAN COOKIES

YIELD: 16 COOKIES | ACTIVE TIME: 40 MINUTES | TOTAL TIME: 2 HOURS

2¼ cups all-purpose flour

14 tablespoons unsalted butter, diced

½ cup caster sugar

2 large egg yolks

2 teaspoons pure vanilla extract

Blue food coloring, gel, or paste, as needed

1 tube black decorating gel

1 tube turquoise decorating gel

1 cup chocolate chips

Apricot jam, warmed, as needed

½ cup orange fondant

1. Place the flour and butter in a food processor and blitz until the mixture is fine crumbs. Add the sugar, egg yolks, and vanilla. Pulse until a smooth dough forms. Divide the dough into two pieces, cover one in plastic wrap, and let it stand at room temperature.

2. Place the dough remaining in the work bowl of the food processor in a mixing bowl, add the blue food coloring, and knead until the food coloring has been incorporated.

3. Place the blue dough between two pieces of parchment paper and roll out until it is ¼-inch thick. Repeat with the uncolored dough that you removed and wrapped in plastic. Keep the pieces of dough between the parchment and refrigerate for 1 hour.

4. Preheat the oven to 375°F and line two large baking sheets with parchment paper. Cut rounds that are 2½ inches in diameter out of the blue dough and place them on the baking sheets. Use a small, snowman-shaped cookie cutter to cut out the center of each round. Repeat with the plain dough. Insert the plain snowmen into the centers in the

blue rounds, and the blue snowmen into the centers of the plain rounds.

5. Bake for about 15 minutes, until the cookies are set. Remove from the oven and briefly let cool on the baking sheets before transferring to a wire rack to cool completely.

6. Decorate the snowmen, using the black icing for the hats, the turquoise icing for scarves, the chocolate chips for eyes, dabs of jam for buttons, and small pieces of the orange fondant, attached via a small dab of jam, for the noses. Let the decorations set before serving.

COCONUT KISSES

2 egg whites

1 pinch kosher salt

2¼ cups confectioners' sugar

14 tablespoons almond paste

1 cup unsweetened shredded coconut

4 teaspoons rum

2 tablespoons fresh lime juice

1. Preheat the oven to 350°F and line two baking sheets with parchment paper. Place the egg whites and salt in a mixing bowl and beat at high speed with a handheld mixer fitted with the whisk attachment until stiff peaks form. Add ¾ cup of the confectioners' sugar and the almond paste, and whisk to incorporate. Fold in another ¾ cup of the confectioners' sugar, the coconut, and the rum.

2. Spoon the dough into a piping bag fitted with a round nozzle, and pipe small mounds onto the baking sheets.

3. Bake for about 20 minutes, until the cookies are set and slightly golden brown. While the cookies are baking, place the remaining confectioners' sugar and the lime juice in a mixing bowl and whisk to combine.

4. Remove the cookies from the oven and let them cool on the baking sheets. Top with the lime glaze and let it set before serving.

PEANUT BUTTER & CHOCOLATE JAM COOKIES

YIELD: 12 COOKIES | ACTIVE TIME: 20 MINUTES | TOTAL TIME: 1 HOUR

1 cup all-purpose flour

½ cup unsweetened cocoa powder

½ teaspoon baking soda

⅛ teaspoon fine-grained sea salt

1 stick unsalted butter, at room temperature and chopped

¾ cup creamy peanut butter, at room temperature

1 cup granulated sugar

½ cup firmly packed light brown sugar

1 egg, at room temperature and beaten

1 teaspoon pure vanilla extract

¼ cup blackberry jam

1. Preheat the oven to 375°F and line two baking sheets with parchment paper. Sift the flour, cocoa powder, baking soda, and salt into a mixing bowl and set it aside.

2. Place the butter, peanut butter, granulated sugar, and brown sugar in a separate mixing bowl. Beat at medium speed with a handheld mixer fitted with the paddle attachment until pale and fluffy, scraping down the sides of the bowl as needed. Add the egg and vanilla, and beat to incorporate. With the handheld mixer running at low speed, gradually add the dry mixture to the wet mixture and beat until a smooth dough forms.

3. Form 2-tablespoon portions of the dough into balls and place them on the baking sheets. Use the handle end of a wooden spoon to make a hole in the center of each ball of dough, about ½-inch deep. Spoon 1 teaspoon of jam into each hole.

4. Bake for 11 to 14 minutes, until the surfaces are cracking. Remove from the oven and let the cookies cool on the baking sheets for 5 minutes before transferring to a wire rack to cool completely.

GREAT FOR GIFTING

Everyone knows that giving is the reason for the season, but the true Christmas greats understand that something homemade, delicious, and beautiful can mean the most.

WHITE CHRISTMAS

YIELD: 16 COOKIES | ACTIVE TIME: 20 MINUTES | TOTAL TIME: 3 HOURS AND 30 MINUTES

4 large egg whites

3 drops pure vanilla extract

1 pinch kosher salt

1¼ cups caster sugar

1. Preheat the oven to 200°F and line two large baking sheets with parchment paper. Place the egg whites, vanilla, and salt in a mixing bowl and beat at high speed with a hand-held mixer fitted with the whisk attachment until soft peaks start to form. Add the caster sugar and beat until stiff peaks form.

2. Transfer the meringue into a piping bag and pipe Christmas tree shapes onto the baking trays.

3. Bake for about 2 hours, until the meringues sound crisp when tapped. Turn the oven off and let the cookies cool in the oven for 1 hour. After 1 hour, carefully peel the cookies off the paper and transfer to wire racks to cool completely.

FROSTED ALMOND & HAZELNUT STARS

YIELD: 24 COOKIES | ACTIVE TIME: 20 MINUTES | TOTAL TIME: 1 HOUR AND 45 MINUTES

1½ cups all-purpose flour, plus more for dusting

⅓ cup almond meal

⅓ cup hazelnut meal

½ cup caster sugar

1 pinch kosher salt

14 tablespoons unsalted butter, chopped

⅓ cup chopped almonds

½ cup confectioners' sugar

Juice of 1 lemon

Sugar stars, for decoration

1. Place the flour, almond meal, hazelnut meal, sugar, and salt in a mixing bowl and stir to combine. Add the butter and work the mixture with a pastry blender until it is coarse crumbs. Knead the mixture with your hands until a smooth dough forms. Incorporate the almonds, form the dough into a ball, cover with plastic wrap, and refrigerate for 1 hour.

2. Preheat the oven to 400°F and line two large baking sheets with parchment paper. Place the dough on a flour-dusted work surface and roll it out into a ¼-inch-thick square. Use cookie cutters to cut the dough into stars and place them on the baking sheet.

3. Bake for about 12 minutes, until golden brown. Remove from the oven and let the cookies cool on the baking sheets for a few minutes before transferring to wire racks to cool completely.

4. Place the confectioners' sugar and lemon juice in a bowl and stir until the frosting has the desired consistency. Spread the frosting over the stars and sprinkle the sugar stars on top. Let the frosting and stars set before serving.

ALMOND MERINGUES

YIELD: 24 COOKIES | ACTIVE TIME: 15 MINUTES | TOTAL TIME: 1 HOUR AND 45 MINUTES

3 egg whites, at room temperature

1 teaspoon pure almond extract

¼ teaspoon kosher salt

⅓ cup granulated sugar

1 tablespoon almond meal

1. Preheat the oven to 250°F and line two baking sheets with parchment paper. Place the egg whites, almond extract, and salt in a mixing bowl and beat at medium speed with a handheld mixer fitted with the whisk attachment until soft peaks form. Incorporate the sugar 1 tablespoon at a time and beat until stiff peaks form.

2. Using a rubber spatula, gently fold in the almond meal. Spoon the meringue mixture into a piping bag fitted with plain tip. Pipe the mixture onto the prepared baking sheets.

3. Bake for 30 minutes, until set. Turn off the oven and allow the meringues to dry in the oven for 45 minutes. Remove the cookie sheets from the oven, gently remove the cookies from the parchment paper, and transfer to wire racks to cool completely.

CHOCOLATE, CRANBERRY & PISTACHIO COOKIES

YIELD: 48 COOKIES | ACTIVE TIME: 10 MINUTES | TOTAL TIME: 45 MINUTES

1 stick unsalted butter, at room temperature

½ cup margarine

1 cup granulated sugar

⅔ cup firmly packed light brown sugar

1 teaspoon baking soda

½ teaspoon kosher salt

2 eggs

1 teaspoon pure vanilla extract

2⅔ cups all-purpose flour

¾ cup semisweet chocolate chips

1 cup dried cranberries

¾ cup shelled pistachios, roughly chopped

1. Preheat oven to 375°F and line two baking sheets with parchment paper. Place the butter, margarine, granulated sugar, and brown sugar in a mixing bowl. Beat at medium speed with a handheld mixer fitted with the paddle attachment until pale and fluffy, scraping down the sides of the bowl as needed. Add the eggs and vanilla, reduce speed to low, and beat to incorporate. Gradually add the flour and beat until a smooth dough forms. Add the chocolate chips, cranberries, and pistachios and fold to incorporate.

2. Place teaspoons of the mixture on the baking sheets and bake for 10 minutes, until the edges start to brown. Remove the cookies from the oven and transfer to wire racks to cool completely.

CHOCOLATE-DIPPED ORANGE COOKIES

Zest and juice of 1 orange

¼ teaspoon powdered saffron

2 sticks unsalted butter, at room temperature

1⅓ cups granulated sugar

1 pinch ground cardamom

1 pinch kosher salt

1 tablespoon light brown sugar

2 egg yolks

2⅓ cups all-purpose flour

¼ cup almond meal

¼ teaspoon baking soda

½ cup orange marmalade

1½ cups dark chocolate chips

1. Preheat the oven to 350°F and line two baking sheets with parchment paper. Place 2 tablespoons of the orange juice in a small saucepan and warm over medium heat. Remove from heat, add the saffron, and stir until dissolved. Set the remaining orange juice aside.

2. Place the butter, granulated sugar, cardamom, salt, brown sugar, and orange zest in a bowl. Beat at medium speed with a hand-held mixer fitted with the paddle attachment until pale and fluffy. Add the egg yolks and beat until incorporated.

3. Sift the flour, almond meal, and baking soda into a separate mixing bowl and whisk to combine. Slowly add the flour mixture and then the saffron-infused orange juice to the to the butter mixture, and beat until thoroughly incorporated.

4. Shape the dough into logs and place in a cookie press or a piping bag fitted with a large tip. Press or pipe 2½-inch-long cookies onto the baking sheets.

5. Bake for about 10 to 12 minutes, until golden brown. Remove from the oven and transfer to wire racks to cool.

6. Place the reserved orange juice and marmalade in a saucepan and bring to a boil. Remove from heat and let cool.

7. Brush the flat side of each cookie with some of the cooled jam and sandwich two cookies together. Let the cookies stand until set.

8. Place the chocolate chips in a microwave-safe bowl and microwave on medium until melted and smooth, removing to stir every 15 seconds. Dip the ends of each cookie into the chocolate and place on waxed paper. Let the chocolate set before serving.

CARDAMOM COOKIES

YIELD: 40 COOKIES | ACTIVE TIME: 15 MINUTES | TOTAL TIME: 1 HOUR

5 tablespoons unsalted butter, at room temperature

⅓ cup granulated sugar

1 pinch lemon zest

1 egg

1 cup all-purpose flour

½ teaspoon ground cardamom

½ cup firmly packed brown sugar

Vanilla sugar, for sprinkling

1. Place the butter, granulated sugar, and lemon zest in a mixing bowl, and beat at medium speed with a handheld mixer fitted with the paddle attachment until pale and fluffy, scraping down the sides of the bowl as needed. Add the egg and beat to incorporate. Sift the flour over the mixture, add the cardamom and brown sugar, and fold to incorporate. Cover the mixing bowl with plastic wrap and refrigerate for 30 minutes.

2. Preheat the oven to 375°F and line two baking sheets with parchment paper. Form teaspoons of the mixture into balls and place them on the baking sheets.

3. Bake for about 12 minutes, until golden brown. Remove from the oven, sprinkle the vanilla sugar on top, and let cool on the baking sheets.

LACE CURTAIN COOKIES

YIELD: 48 COOKIES | ACTIVE TIME: 15 MINUTES | TOTAL TIME: 1 HOUR AND 45 MINUTES

5 cups all-purpose flour, plus more for dusting

1½ teaspoons baking powder

1 teaspoon kosher salt

2 sticks unsalted butter, at room temperature

2 cups granulated sugar

2 teaspoons pure vanilla extract

2 large eggs, lightly beaten

Confectioners' sugar, for dusting

1. Sift the flour, baking powder, and salt into a large mixing bowl. Place the butter, granulated sugar, and vanilla in a separate mixing bowl, and beat at medium speed with a handheld mixer fitted with the paddle attachment until pale and fluffy, scraping down the sides of the bowl as needed. Add the beaten eggs and beat until incorporated. Gradually add the dry mixture and work the mixture with your hands until a smooth dough forms. Shape the dough into a ball, cover with plastic wrap, and refrigerate for 1 hour.

2. Preheat oven to 325°F and line two baking sheets with parchment paper. Divide the chilled dough into four pieces. Place one piece on a flour-dusted work surface and roll out to ⅛-inch thick. Use corrugated nesting lace cookie cutters to cut the dough into cookies and place them on the prepared baking sheets. Repeat with the remaining pieces of dough.

3. Bake for about 10 minutes, until the edges have browned. Remove from the oven and transfer the cookies to wire racks to cool completely. Dust with confectioners' sugar before serving.

NUTTY STAR CLUSTERS

2¼ cups all-purpose flour, plus more for dusting

1½ cups caster sugar

1½ cups almond meal

1 teaspoon orange zest

2½ sticks unsalted butter, chilled and divided into tablespoons

1 large egg

1 teaspoon pure vanilla extract

1¼ cups red currant jam

1 tube white decorating gel, as needed

1. Place the flour, sugar, almond meal, and orange zest in a large mixing bowl and stir to combine. Create a well in the center and place the butter around the edge of the well. Crack the egg into the well and add the vanilla extract. Work the mixture with a pastry blender until it is coarse crumbs. Knead the mixture with your hands until a smooth dough forms. Cover the dough with plastic wrap and refrigerate for 45 minutes.

2. Preheat the oven to 375°F and line two baking sheets with parchment paper. Place the dough on a flour-dusted work surface and roll it out to ⅛-inch thick. Use cookie cutters to cut into various sizes of star shapes and place them on the baking sheets.

3. Bake for 12 to 15 minutes, until they are golden brown and dry to the touch. Remove from the oven and let cool on the baking sheets.

4. Place the jam in a saucepan and warm over medium heat. Spread the warm jam over the cookies and let the jam set. Let the jam set before decorating the edges with the white gel.

TOFFEE & PECAN STARS

YIELD: 24 COOKIES | ACTIVE TIME: 15 MINUTES | TOTAL TIME: 2 HOURS

1⅔ cups all-purpose flour, plus more for dusting

6 tablespoons cornstarch

¼ teaspoon kosher salt

1½ sticks unsalted butter, at room temperature

⅓ cup granulated sugar

3 tablespoons light brown sugar

2 teaspoons pure vanilla extract

⅓ cup semisweet chocolate chips

1 cup chopped pecans

1 cup toffee pieces

Confectioners' sugar, for sprinkling

1. Place the flour, cornstarch, and salt in a mixing bowl, whisk to combine, and set aside. Place the butter, granulated sugar, brown sugar, and vanilla in a separate mixing bowl. Beat at medium speed with a handheld mixer fitted with the paddle attachment until pale and fluffy, scraping down the sides of the bowl as needed. Reduce speed to low, add the flour mixture, chocolate chips, pecans, and toffee bits, and beat until a smooth dough forms. Cover the dough in plastic wrap and refrigerate for 1 hour.

2. Preheat the oven to 350°F and line two baking sheets with parchment paper. Place one piece on a flour-dusted work surface and roll out to ¼-inch thick. Use cookie cutters to cut the dough into star shapes and place them on the baking sheets.

3. Bake, rotating the sheets halfway through, for 12 minutes, until the edges are golden brown. Remove from the oven and briefly let the cookies cool on the baking sheets before transferring to a wire rack to cool completely. Dust with confectioners' sugar before serving.

TERRACE COOKIES

YIELD: 15 COOKIES | ACTIVE TIME: 20 MINUTES | TOTAL TIME: 2 HOURS AND 45 MINUTES

2¼ cups all-purpose flour, plus more for dusting

⅔ cup granulated sugar

14 tablespoons unsalted butter, chilled and minced

1 egg

½ cup red currant jam

1. Place the flour, sugar, and salt in a mixing bowl and stir to combine. Make a well in the center of the mixture and dot the edge of the well with the butter. Crack the egg into the well and work the mixture with your hands until a smooth dough forms. Cover in plastic wrap and refrigerate for 2 hours.

2. Preheat the oven to 375°F and line two baking sheets with parchment paper. Place the dough on a flour-dusted work surface and roll it out to ¼-inch thick. Use cookie cutters to cut dough into desired shapes, varying the sizes of each shape and cutting the same number of cookies with each cookie cutter. Place the cookies on the baking sheets.

3. Bake for about 8 minutes, until golden brown. Remove the cookies from the oven and briefly let them cool on the baking sheets.

4. Place the jam in a saucepan and warm over medium heat, stirring until it is smooth. Spread the jam on the large and medium-sized cookies and stack the latter on top of the former. Stack the smallest cookies on top, top with a little more jam, and let the cookies cool completely before serving.

CARAMEL CREAM SANDWICH COOKIES

YIELD: 24 COOKIES | ACTIVE TIME: 30 MINUTES | TOTAL TIME: 2 HOURS

For the Cookies

10 tablespoons
unsalted butter, at
room temperature

6 tablespoons
confectioners' sugar

3 tablespoons vanilla
sugar

2⅓ cups all-purpose
flour, plus more for
dusting

2 teaspoons cornstarch

**For the Caramel
Cream**

1⅓ cups granulated
sugar, plus 2
tablespoons

1 stick unsalted
butter, at room
temperature

9 tablespoons heavy
whipping cream

1. To begin preparations for the cookies, place the butter and sugars in a mixing bowl, and beat at medium speed with a handheld mixer fitted with the paddle attachment until pale and fluffy, scraping down the sides of the bowl as needed. Sift the flour and cornstarch over the mixture, and knead it with your hands until a smooth dough forms. Cover the dough in plastic wrap and refrigerate for 30 minutes.

2. Preheat oven to 350°F and line two baking sheets with parchment paper. Divide the dough into three portions. Working with one piece at a time, place the dough on a flour-dusted work surface and roll out to ⅛-inch thick. Cut the dough into rounds and place them on the baking sheets. Bake for about 8 minutes, until the edges start to brown. Remove from the oven and transfer to wire racks to cool completely.

3. To prepare the caramel cream, place the 2 tablespoons sugar in a small saucepan and cook over medium heat until sugar is dissolved and golden brown. Remove from heat and set aside. Place the remaining sugar, butter, and cream in a medium saucepan

and cook over medium heat, stirring constantly, until mixture comes to a boil. Stir in the caramelized sugar, return to a boil, and cook for 2 minutes, stirring constantly. Remove from heat and beat until thick and creamy.

4. Spoon the caramel cream into a piping bag fitted with a serrated tip and pipe onto the underside of each cookie. Gently sandwich the cookie halves together and serve.

SILVER SHELL BISCUITS

YIELD: 36 COOKIES | ACTIVE TIME: 15 MINUTES | TOTAL TIME: 40 MINUTES

1 cup all-purpose flour

1 tablespoon cornstarch

1 teaspoon baking powder

7 tablespoons unsalted butter

¼ cup caster sugar

1 tablespoon vanilla sugar

1 pinch kosher salt

36 silver sugar pearls

1. Preheat the oven to 350°F and line two baking sheets with parchment paper. Place the flour, cornstarch, and baking powder in a mixing bowl and stir to combine. Place the butter, granulated sugar, vanilla sugar, and salt in a separate mixing bowl and beat at medium speed with a handheld mixer fitted with the paddle attachment until pale and fluffy, scraping down the sides of the bowl as needed. With the mixer running at low speed, gradually add the dry mixture and beat until a smooth dough forms.

2. Roll the dough into a log that is about 2 inches in diameter and slice it into ¼-inch-thick rounds. Press with cookie stamps and place them on the baking sheets. Bake for about 5 minutes, until they are a light golden brown. Remove from the oven, press a silver sugar pearl into the center of each cookie, and transfer to wire racks to cool.

ICY & SPICY STARS

YIELD: 36 COOKIES | ACTIVE TIME: 20 MINUTES | TOTAL TIME: 1 HOUR AND 15 MINUTES

2½ cups almond meal

1 tablespoon cinnamon

Zest of 1 lemon

3 egg whites

⅛ teaspoon kosher salt

2¾ cups confectioners' sugar, plus more for dusting

1¾ teaspoons fresh lemon juice

1. Preheat oven to 325°F and line two baking sheets with parchment paper. Place the almond meal, cinnamon, and lemon zest in a mixing bowl and stir to combine. Place the egg whites and salt in a separate mixing bowl, and beat at high speed with a hand-held mixer fitted with the whisk attachment until soft peaks form. With the mixer running, slowly sift the confectioners' sugar over the mixture. Beat until stiff peaks form. Reserve ⅓ cup of the egg white mixture. Add the almond meal mixture to the remaining egg white mixture and fold to incorporate.

2. Dust a work surface with the confectioners' sugar, place the dough on it, and roll the dough out to ¼-inch thick. Use cookie cutters to cut the dough into star shapes and place them on the baking sheets.

3. Bake for 20 minutes, until they are a light golden brown and still soft in the center. Remove from the oven and transfer to wire racks to cool.

4. Add the lemon juice to the reserved egg white mixture and stir to combine. Brush the tops of the cookies lightly with the glaze and let it set before serving.

THE PARTY CIRCUIT

One of the great things about Christmas is that people are always getting together and taking comfort in one another's presence while enjoying various treats. These cookies have the elegance to stand out on any dessert table and the flavor to back up that intrigue.

COCONUT & LEMON SANDWICH COOKIES

YIELD: 24 COOKIES | ACTIVE TIME: 20 MINUTES | TOTAL TIME: 3 HOURS AND 30 MINUTES

For the Cookies

1 cup unsweetened shredded coconut

2 sticks unsalted butter, at room temperature

⅓ cup granulated sugar

Zest of 1 lemon

1 teaspoon lemon oil

2 cups all-purpose flour

½ teaspoon kosher salt

For the Filling

1 cup confectioners' sugar

4 tablespoons unsalted butter

Zest and juice of 1 lemon

2 tablespoons light corn syrup

1. Preheat the oven to 325°F. To begin preparations for the cookies, place the coconut on a baking sheet, place it in the oven, and toast, while rotating halfway through, until lightly browned, about 10 to 12 minutes.

2. Place the butter, sugar, lemon zest, and lemon oil in a mixing bowl, and beat at medium speed with a handheld mixer fitted with the paddle attachment until light and fluffy. Slowly add the flour and salt, and beat until a soft dough forms. Add the toasted coconut and beat until incorporated.

3. Place the dough on a sheet of waxed paper and form it into a 2½-inch-thick log. Cover with plastic wrap and refrigerate for 2 hours.

4. Preheat the oven to 350°F and line two baking sheets with parchment paper. Cut the dough into ¼-inch-thick slices and place them on the baking sheets. Bake for about 10 minutes, until the edges start to brown. Remove from the oven and let the cookies cool on the baking sheets for 2 minutes before transferring them to wire racks to cool completely.

5. To prepare the filling, place all of the ingredients in a mixing bowl, and beat with a handheld mixer fitted with the paddle attachment until the mixture is light and fluffy.

6. Spread approximately 1 teaspoon of the filling on a cookie and top with another cookie. Repeat until all of the cookies and filling have been used. Refrigerate for 15 minutes before serving.

CHOCOLATE-DIPPED MACADAMIA & COCONUT TRIANGLES

YIELD: 18 COOKIES | ACTIVE TIME: 45 MINUTES | TOTAL TIME: 1 HOUR AND 45 MINUTES

1 cup all-purpose flour, plus 2 tablespoons

⅔ cup firmly packed light brown sugar, plus 1 tablespoon

½ teaspoon kosher salt

5 tablespoons unsalted butter, chilled and chopped

2 tablespoons honey

1 teaspoon pure vanilla extract

1 large egg

1 cup unsalted macadamia nuts, chopped

1 cup shredded unsweetened coconut

⅔ cup semisweet chocolate chips

1. Preheat the oven to 375°F and line a 9-inch baking dish with aluminum foil. Grease the foil with nonstick cooking spray.

2. Place the 1 cup flour, 1 tablespoon brown sugar, and the salt in a mixing bowl and whisk to combine. Add the butter and work the mixture with a pastry blender until it is coarse crumbs. Press the mixture into the baking dish and bake for about 10 minutes, until the edges are golden brown.

3. While the crust is baking, place the remaining flour and brown sugar, honey, vanilla, and egg in a mixing bowl and beat until combined. Add the macadamia nuts and coconut, and stir until evenly distributed.

4. Gently spread the macadamia-and-coconut topping over the warm crust. Return to the oven and bake until the topping is a light golden brown and the edges pull away from the sides of the pan, about 15 minutes. Remove and let cool completely in the pan.

5. Cut into 3-inch squares and then cut each square in half. Place the chocolate chips in a microwave-safe bowl and microwave on medium until melted and smooth, removing to stir every 15 seconds. Dip one corner of each triangle in the melted chocolate and place each cookie on pieces of waxed paper. Let the chocolate set before serving.

ALMOND COOKIES

YIELD: 18 COOKIES | ACTIVE TIME: 15 MINUTES | TOTAL TIME: 1 HOUR

¼ cup all-purpose flour

½ cup confectioners' sugar

½ cup granulated sugar

2 egg whites

½ pound unsweetened almond paste

½ cup slivered almonds

1. Preheat the oven to 350°F and line two baking sheets with parchment paper. Place the flour, confectioners' sugar, granulated sugar, egg whites, and almond paste in a large mixing bowl and work the mixture with your hands until an extremely sticky dough forms.

2. Place the almonds in a bowl. Place teaspoons of the dough in the bowl of almonds and roll the pieces of dough until completely coated. Place on the baking sheets.

3. Bake for about 15 minutes, until golden brown. Remove and let cool on the baking sheets for a few minutes before transferring to a wire rack to cool completely.

MERINGUE SNOWFLAKES

YIELD: 36 COOKIES | ACTIVE TIME: 15 MINUTES | TOTAL TIME: 1 HOUR AND 15 MINUTES

3 egg whites

1 tablespoon fresh lemon juice

1 pinch kosher salt

1¼ cups confectioners' sugar, plus more for dusting

1. Preheat the oven to 250°F and line a baking sheet with parchment paper. Place the egg whites, lemon juice, and salt in a mixing bowl, and beat at medium speed with a handheld mixer fitted with the whisk attachment until soft peaks form. Gradually add the confectioners' sugar and beat the mixture until stiff peaks form and it is glossy.

2. Spoon the mixture into a piping bag fitted with a thin, smooth nozzle and pipe snowflake shapes onto the baking sheet. Bake until dry to the touch, about 40 minutes. Turn off the oven, open the door, and let the snowflakes cool completely in the oven. Remove from the oven and dust with additional confectioners' sugar before serving.

HAZELNUT CHEWIES

YIELD: 40 COOKIES | ACTIVE TIME: 20 MINUTES | TOTAL TIME: 1 HOUR AND 45 MINUTES

3¼ cups all-purpose flour

½ teaspoon kosher salt

2 teaspoons baking powder

2 cups Nutella

4 tablespoons unsalted butter, at room temperature

2 cups granulated sugar

1 teaspoon pure vanilla extract

1 teaspoon instant espresso powder

2 large eggs

5 tablespoons milk

1 cup hazelnuts, toasted and minced

1¼ cups confectioners' sugar

1. Whisk together flour, salt, and baking powder in a mixing bowl. Place the Nutella, butter, and granulated sugar in a separate mixing bowl, and beat at medium speed with a handheld mixer fitted with the paddle attachment until pale and fluffy, scraping down the sides of the bowl as needed. Add the vanilla, espresso powder, and eggs, and beat until thoroughly combined. Reduce speed to low, add the flour mixture and the milk. Beat until the dough just holds together. Fold in half of the hazelnuts, cover the dough with plastic wrap, and refrigerate for 1 hour.

2. Preheat oven to 375°F and line two baking sheets with parchment paper. Place the remaining hazelnuts in a bowl. Place the confectioners' sugar in another bowl. Form tablespoons of the dough into balls, roll them in the hazelnuts, and then roll them in the confectioners' sugar. Place them on the baking sheets.

3. Bake for about 8 minutes, until set. Remove from the oven and let the cookies cool on the baking sheets for 5 minutes before transferring them to wire racks to cool completely.

GOLD STARS

3 egg whites

4½ cups confectioners' sugar, sifted, plus more as needed

3¼ cups almond meal, plus more as needed

1 tablespoon cinnamon

1 pinch kosher salt

Hot water (125°F), as needed

Edible gold dust, for decoration

1. Preheat the oven to 300°F and line two baking sheets with parchment paper. Place the egg whites in a large mixing bowl. Beat at high speed with a handheld mixer fitted with the whisk attachment until stiff peaks form. Add half of the confectioners' sugar and stir until fully incorporated. Fold in the almond meal, 2 teaspoons of the cinnamon, and salt. Work the mixture until a stiff but pliable dough forms. If the dough is too soft, stir in additional almond meal.

2. Place the dough on a work surface that has been dusted with confectioners' sugar. Roll it out to ⅓-inch thick. Use cookie cutters to cut the dough into star shapes and place them on the baking sheets.

3. Bake for about 15 minutes, until the edges are set. Remove from the oven and let the cookies cool on the baking sheets.

4. Place the remaining confectioners' sugar and cinnamon in a mixing bowl. Stir in hot water until the frosting achieves the desired consistency. Spread the frosting on the cookies, sprinkle the gold dust on top, and let set before serving.

CHOCOLATE MERINGUES WITH PINE NUTS & PINK PEPPERCORNS

YIELD: 20 COOKIES | ACTIVE TIME: 20 MINUTES | TOTAL TIME: 3 HOURS AND 30 MINUTES

½ cup caster sugar

1 tablespoon unsweetened cocoa powder

2 large egg whites

1 pinch kosher salt

½ teaspoon cream of tartar

⅓ cup pine nuts

1 tablespoon pink peppercorns, lightly crushed

1. Preheat the oven to 250°F and line two baking sheets with parchment paper. Place the sugar and cocoa powder in a mixing bowl and whisk to combine. Place the egg whites and salt in a separate mixing bowl, and beat at high speed with a handheld mixer fitted with the whisk attachment until stiff peaks form. Add the cream of tartar and beat until incorporated. Incorporate the sugar mixture 1 tablespoon at a time, and beat the mixture until it is thick and glossy.

2. Spoon the mixture into a piping bag fitted with star-shaped nozzle. Pipe the meringue onto the baking sheets and dot each one with pine nuts and crushed peppercorns.

3. Bake for about 1 hour and 45 minutes, until the meringues are dry and hollow sounding when tapped lightly. Turn off the oven, open the oven door, and let the meringues cool in the oven for 1 hour. After 1 hour, remove from the oven and transfer to wire racks to cool completely.

VANILLA & STRAWBERRY SANDWICH COOKIES

YIELD: 24 COOKIES | ACTIVE TIME: 1 HOUR | TOTAL TIME: 2 HOURS AND 15 MINUTES

For the Cookies

14 tablespoons unsalted butter, at room temperature

⅓ cup granulated sugar

2 tablespoons vanilla sugar

1 teaspoon orange zest

3 eggs

½ teaspoon baking powder

1 pinch ground anise

1 pinch cinnamon

1 pinch ground cloves

½ cup hazelnut meal

1⅔ cups all-purpose flour

Milk, as needed

Confectioners' sugar, for dusting

1. To begin preparations for the cookies, place the butter, granulated sugar, and vanilla sugar in a mixing bowl, and beat at medium speed with a handheld mixer fitted with the paddle attachment until pale and fluffy, scraping down the sides of the bowl as needed. Add the orange zest and eggs and beat to incorporate.

2. Place the baking powder, spices, nuts, and flour in a separate mixing bowl and stir to combine. With the handheld mixer running at low speed, gradually add the dry mixture to the wet mixture, and beat until a smooth dough forms. If the dough is too sticky, incorporate milk in 1-teaspoon increments. Cover the dough in plastic wrap and refrigerate for 30 minutes.

3. Preheat the oven to 350°F and line two large baking sheets with parchment paper. Place the dough in a piping bag fitted with a serrated nozzle and pipe little dots onto the baking sheets. Refrigerate for another 30 minutes.

4. Bake for about 12 minutes, until lightly browned. Remove from the oven and let the cookies cool on the baking sheets. Dust with the confectioners' sugar and set aside.

For the Filling

2¼ cups milk

Seeds and pod of 1 vanilla bean

5 egg yolks

⅔ cup granulated sugar

1 pinch kosher salt

2½ tablespoons all-purpose flour or cornstarch

1 cup strawberry jam

5. To prepare the filling, place the milk, vanilla seeds, and the vanilla bean pod in a saucepan, and bring to a boil. Place the egg yolks, sugar, and salt in a separate bowl, and stir until combined. Incorporate the flour or cornstarch. Then gradually add half of the hot milk into the mixture, stirring constantly. Place the tempered egg mixture in the saucepan, reduce the heat to low, and remove the vanilla pod. Stir constantly until the mixture is thick enough to coat the back of a spoon, making sure it does not come to a boil. Remove from heat and let cool.

6. To assemble the cookies, spread some of the cream on one cookie, top with some jam, and place another cookie on top. Let the cookies set before serving.

CRISPY WREATH COOKIES

YIELD: 12 COOKIES | ACTIVE TIME: 30 MINUTES | TOTAL TIME: 1 HOUR AND 45 MINUTES

1¾ cups all-purpose flour, plus more for dusting

½ teaspoon kosher salt

9 tablespoons unsalted butter, at room temperature

½ cup caster sugar

1 large egg yolk

1½ teaspoons pure vanilla extract

1 cup almond meal

⅔ cup white chocolate chips

1 cup shelled and chopped pistachios

½ cup dried cranberries, chopped

1. Place the flour and salt in a large mixing bowl and stir to combine. Place the butter and sugar in a separate mixing bowl, and beat at medium speed with a handheld mixer fitted with the paddle attachment until pale and fluffy, scraping down the sides of the bowl as needed. Add the egg yolk and vanilla, and beat to incorporate. With the handheld mixer running at low speed, gradually add the flour mixture and the almond meal. Beat until a smooth dough forms. Cover the dough in plastic wrap, flatten it into a disk, and refrigerate for 30 minutes.

2. Preheat the oven to 350°F and line two large baking sheets with parchment paper. Place the dough on a flour-dusted work surface, and roll it out to ¼-inch thick. Use cookie cutters to cut out rounds from the dough and then use smaller cookie cutters to cut out the centers of the rounds. Place the cookies on the baking sheets.

3. Bake for about 15 minutes, until set and a light golden brown. Remove from the oven and let the cookies cool on the baking sheets for 5 minutes before transferring them to wire racks to cool completely.

4. Place the white chocolate chips in a microwave-safe bowl and microwave on medium until melted and smooth, removing to stir every 15 seconds. Drizzle the melted chocolate over the cookies and scatter the pistachios and cranberries on top. Let the chocolate set before serving.

MACARONS

3 egg whites

¼ cup granulated sugar

1⅔ cups confectioners' sugar

1 cup almond meal

2 to 3 drops of preferred gel food coloring

1. Line a baking sheet with parchment paper. Place the egg whites in a mixing bowl, and beat at high speed with a handheld mixer fitted with the whisk attachment until foamy. Add the granulated sugar and continue to beat until the mixture is glossy, fluffy, and holds soft peaks.

2. Sift the confectioners' sugar and ground almonds into a separate bowl. Add this mixture and the gel food coloring into the egg white mixture. Fold until incorporated, taking care not to overmix the batter.

3. Transfer the batter into a plastic bag with one corner removed. Pipe a 1½-inch disk of batter onto the parchment-lined baking sheet. If the disk holds a peak instead of flattening immediately, gently fold the batter a few more times and retest. Repeat until the disk flattens into an even disk. Transfer the batter into a piping bag.

4. Pipe the batter onto the parchment-lined baking sheet. Let stand at room temperature until a skin forms on top, about 1 hour.

5. Preheat the oven to 275°F. Place the cookies in the oven and bake until they are set but not browned, about 10 minutes. Remove and let cool completely before filling. See page 153 for tips on what to fill them with.

MACARON FILLINGS

Chocolate Ganache: Heat ½ cup heavy cream in a saucepan and bring to a simmer. Stir in ¼ pound of chopped dark chocolate and continue stirring until the chocolate is melted. Add 2 tablespoons of unsalted butter, stir until the mixture is smooth, and chill in the refrigerator until thick and cool.

Vanilla Buttercream: Place 10 tablespoons unsalted butter in a mixing bowl, and beat at medium speed with a handheld mixer fitted with a whisk attachment until smooth. Add 1½ teaspoons pure vanilla extract, 1¼ cups confectioners' sugar, and a pinch of kosher salt and beat until the mixture is fully combined. Scrape down the bowl as needed while mixing. Add 1 tablespoon heavy cream and beat until the mixture is light and fluffy, about 4 minutes, stopping to scrape down the bowl as needed.

Raspberry Buttercream: Add ¼ cup of seedless raspberry jam to the Vanilla Buttercream and beat until incorporated.

CHOCOLATE-COVERED CHERRY COOKIES

YIELD: 48 COOKIES | ACTIVE TIME: 25 MINUTES | TOTAL TIME: 45 MINUTES

For the Cookies

1 stick unsalted butter

1 cup granulated sugar

1 egg

1½ teaspoons pure vanilla extract

1¼ cups all-purpose flour

2 oz. unsweetened cocoa powder

1 pinch kosher salt

½ teaspoon baking powder

½ teaspoon baking soda

48 maraschino cherries, stems removed, patted dry

1 cup semisweet chocolate chips

½ cup sweetened condensed milk

1 tablespoon maraschino cherry syrup

1. To begin preparations for the cookies, preheat the oven to 350°F and line two large baking sheets with parchment paper. Place the butter and sugar in a mixing bowl, and beat at medium speed with a handheld mixer fitted with the paddle attachment until pale and fluffy, scraping down the sides of the bowl as needed. Add the egg and vanilla, reduce speed to low, and beat to incorporate. Place the flour, cocoa powder, salt, baking powder, and baking soda in a separate mixing bowl and whisk to combine. With the handheld mixer running at low speed, gradually add the dry mixture to the wet mixture and beat until a smooth dough forms.

2. Shape tablespoons of the dough into balls and place them on the baking sheets. Gently push one cherry halfway into each ball.

3. Place the chocolate chips and condensed milk in a microwave-safe bowl and microwave on medium until the chocolate is melted and the mixture is smooth, removing to stir every 15 seconds. When the chocolate is melted, stir in the cherry juice and spoon the mixture over the cookies.

For the Icing

6 tablespoons unsalted butter, melted

1 cup confectioners' sugar

1½ teaspoons pure vanilla extract

2½ tablespoons hot water (125°F)

4. Bake for about 10 minutes, until the edges are set. Remove from the oven and let them cool on the baking sheets. While the cookies are cooling, prepare the icing. Place the butter, confectioners' sugar, and vanilla in a bowl, and gradually incorporate hot water until the icing achieves the desired consistency. Spoon the icing into a piping bag fitted with a fine, decorative tip and pipe snowflake shapes onto the cookies. Let the icing set before serving.

AROUND THE WORLD

As Christmas brings joy to people the world over, a number of tasty confections from numerous cultures have made their way into the holiday cookie canon.

POLVORONES

2 sticks unsalted butter, at room temperature

1¾ cups confectioners' sugar

1 cup cake flour, plus more for dusting

1 cup self-rising flour

1 cup almonds, blanched and minced

½ teaspoon pure vanilla extract

Warm water (110°F), as needed

1. Preheat the oven to 350°F and line two baking sheets with parchment paper. Place the butter and 1¼ cups of the confectioners' sugar in a mixing bowl, and beat at medium speed with a handheld mixer fitted with the paddle attachment until light and fluffy. Add the flours, almonds, and vanilla, and beat until the dough is just holding together and very stiff. Add a few drops of warm water, if necessary, to make it pliable.

2. Form tablespoons of the dough into balls, place them on the baking sheets, and flatten them slightly with the bottom of a glass that has been dipped in flour. Bake until lightly browned, about 10 minutes. Remove from the oven.

3. Sift the remaining sugar into a shallow dish and use a spatula to transfer the cookies to the bowl. Roll the cookies in the sugar until they are evenly coated and then transfer them to wire racks to cool completely.

APRICOT KOLACHES

½ **pound dried apricots**

½ **cup granulated sugar**

10 **tablespoons all-purpose flour, plus more for dusting**

¼ **teaspoon kosher salt**

½ **cup cream cheese, at room temperature**

1 **stick unsalted butter, at room temperature**

¼ **cup confectioners' sugar, for dusting**

1. Place the dried apricots in a saucepan and cover with water. Bring the water to a boil over medium-high heat. Cook until the apricots are soft, adding more water if too much evaporates. Add the sugar and reduce the heat so that the mixture simmers. Cook, stirring to dissolve the sugar, until the liquid thickens into a syrup. Transfer the mixture to a blender or a food processor and puree until smooth. Let stand until cool.

2. Sift the flour and salt into a mixing bowl. Using a handheld mixer fitted with the paddle attachment, beat the cream cheese and butter on high until the mixture is fluffy. Gradually add the dry mixture to the wet mixture and beat to incorporate. Divide the dough into two balls and cover loosely with plastic wrap. Flatten each ball to about ¾-inch thick and refrigerate until the dough is firm, about 2 hours.

3. Preheat the oven to 375°F and line a large baking sheet with parchment paper. Place one of the balls of dough on a flour-dusted work surface and roll it out into a ⅛-inch-thick square. Cut the dough into as many 1½-inch squares as possible.

4. Place approximately 1 teaspoon of the apricot mixture in the center of each square. Gently lift two opposite corners of each square and fold one over the other. Gently press down to seal and transfer to the baking sheet.

5. Bake for 12 to 14 minutes, until the cookies are golden brown. Remove, briefly let them cool on the baking sheets, and transfer to a wire rack to cool completely. Repeat with the remaining ball of dough. When all of the kolaches have been baked and cooled, dust with the confectioners' sugar.

FIORI DI MANDORLE

YIELD: 24 COOKIES | ACTIVE TIME: 20 MINUTES | TOTAL TIME: 1 HOUR

3 cups almond meal

2 cups confectioners' sugar, plus more for dusting

Zest of 1 lemon

2 large eggs, lightly beaten

1 tablespoon milk

24 Luxardo maraschino cherries

1. Preheat the oven to 350°F and line two baking sheets with parchment paper. Place the almond meal, confectioners' sugar, and lemon zest in a large mixing bowl and stir to combine. Add the egg and milk, and work the mixture with your hands until a soft, slightly sticky dough forms.

2. Dust your hands with confectioners' sugar and then roll tablespoons of the dough into balls. Place them on the baking sheets and dust them with additional confectioners' sugar. Make an indent with your thumb in each piece of dough and fill with a cocktail cherry.

3. Bake for about 18 minutes, until golden brown and dry to the touch. Remove from the oven and transfer to wire racks to cool completely.

LINZER BARS

YIELD: 30 BARS | ACTIVE TIME: 40 MINUTES | TOTAL TIME: 2 HOURS

2 sticks unsalted butter, at room temperature

1½ cups granulated sugar

1 teaspoon baking powder

½ teaspoon kosher salt

1 egg

Seeds from 1 vanilla bean

1 teaspoon pure almond extract

3⅓ cups all-purpose flour

1 cup minced almonds

1 cup raspberry jam

9 tablespoons confectioners' sugar

½ teaspoon pure almond extract

1 to 2 tablespoons milk

1. Preheat the oven to 300°F and line a baking sheet with parchment paper. Place the butter in a mixing bowl, and beat at medium speed with a handheld mixer fitted with the paddle attachment until pale and fluffy. Add the sugar, baking powder, salt, and egg, and beat to incorporate. Add the vanilla seeds and half of the almond extract, and stir to incorporate. Sift the flour over the mixture and knead the mixture with your hands until a soft, smooth dough forms.

2. Divide the dough into three pieces and shape each one into a 10-inch log. Roll each log in the almonds and place them on the baking sheet. Gently flatten each log to a thickness of about 1 inch. Using the back of a spoon, create a furrow about ½-inch deep and 1-inch wide down the middle of each log.

3. Bake for about 30 minutes, until the edges are lightly browned. Remove from the oven and let the logs cool on the baking sheet for 5 minutes before transferring them to a wire rack to cool completely. You may have to reshape the furrows as the logs start to cool.

4. Place the jam in a saucepan and warm over medium heat, stirring until smooth. Spoon the jam into the furrows and allow it to set.

5. Place the confectioners' sugar and remaining almond extract in a mixing bowl and stir to combine. Gradually incorporate the milk until the frosting achieves the desired consistency. Drizzle the frosting over the logs and let it set before cutting them into bars and serving.

FLORENTINES

YIELD: 30 COOKIES | ACTIVE TIME: 10 MINUTES | TOTAL TIME: 45 MINUTES

¾ **cup granulated sugar**

1 teaspoon pure vanilla extract

7 tablespoons heavy cream

3 tablespoons unsalted butter

1½ cups sliced almonds

⅓ cup candied citrus peels

⅓ cup dried cherries or plums, chopped

⅓ cup raisins

1¼ cups dark chocolate chips

1. Place the sugar, vanilla extract, and cream in a saucepan and bring to a boil. Remove from heat, add the butter, and let it melt. Stir in the almonds, candied citrus peels, dried cherries or plums, and raisins.

2. Preheat the oven to 400°F and line two baking sheets with parchment paper. Place teaspoons of the mixture on the baking sheets, place the cookies in the oven, and bake for 5 to 10 minutes, until golden brown. Remove from the oven and let the cookies cool on the baking sheets for 5 minutes before transferring to wire racks to cool completely.

3. Place the chocolate chips in a microwave-safe bowl. Microwave on medium until melted and smooth, removing to stir every 15 seconds. Spread the melted chocolate on the undersides of the florentines and leave to set before serving.

YIN & YANG WAFERS

YIELD: 48 COOKIES | ACTIVE TIME: 30 MINUTES | TOTAL TIME: 2 HOURS

2⅔ cups all-purpose
flour, plus more for
dusting

1½ sticks
unsalted butter, at
room temperature

1¼ cups confectioners'
sugar

2 egg yolks

½ teaspoon pure
vanilla extract

2 tablespoons
unsweetened cocoa
powder

1. Sift the flour into a mixing bowl. Place the butter and confectioners' sugar in a separate mixing bowl, and beat with a handheld mixer fitted with the paddle attachment and at medium speed until pale and fluffy, scraping down the bowl as needed. Add the eggs and vanilla, reduce speed to low, and beat to incorporate. Gradually add the flour and beat until the dough just holds together.

2. Divide the dough in two and set one aside. Add the cocoa powder to the other dough and beat on low speed until thoroughly incorporated. Place the chocolate dough on a flour-dusted work surface and roll it into a 10-inch log that is about 1½ inches in diameter. Repeat with the other half of the dough. Cover the logs in plastic wrap and refrigerate for 30 minutes.

3. Press the handle of a long wooden spoon into one side of the chocolate dough, making an indent along its length. Roll handle into and then away from log, creating an apostrophe shape. Repeat with vanilla log. Fit logs together and press lightly to seal. Gently roll into a 2-inch diameter log. Cover in plastic wrap and freeze for 30 minutes.

4. Preheat the oven to 350°F and line two baking sheets with parchment paper. Place the dough on a piece of parchment, cut into ¼-inch-thick rounds, and place them on the baking sheets.

5. Bake for about 10 minutes, until the cookies are firm. Remove from the oven and transfer to wire racks to cool completely.

ELISEN GINGERBREAD

YIELD: 20 COOKIES | ACTIVE TIME: 30 MINUTES | TOTAL TIME: 7 HOURS AND 30 MINUTES

3 large eggs

1½ cups caster sugar

1 pinch ground cloves

1 teaspoon cinnamon

½ teaspoon baking powder

Zest of 1 lemon

¼ cup chopped dried fruit

3 cups almond meal

1 cup dark chocolate chips

1. Line two to three large baking sheets with parchment paper. Place the eggs and sugar in a mixing bowl, and beat at medium speed with a handheld mixer fitted with the whisk attachment until pale and fluffy. Add the spices, baking powder, and lemon zest, and whisk to incorporate. Fold in the dried fruit, add the almond meal, and stir until a smooth dough forms. Place 2-tablespoon portions of the dough on the baking sheets and smooth the tops with a rubber spatula. Let the cookies sit at room temperature for 6 hours.

2. Preheat the oven to 325°F. Place the cookies in the oven and bake for about 20 minutes, until browned and slightly puffy. Remove from the oven and transfer to wire racks to cool completely.

3. Place the chocolate chips in a microwave-safe bowl and microwave on medium until melted and smooth, removing to stir every 15 seconds. Spoon the melted chocolate over the cookies and let it set before serving.

LEBKUCHEN

YIELD: 30 COOKIES | ACTIVE TIME: 20 MINUTES | TOTAL TIME: 1 HOUR

1¼ cups hazelnuts, toasted

1 cup almonds, toasted

¾ cup granulated sugar

1½ teaspoons cinnamon

½ teaspoon ground cardamom

½ teaspoon grated nutmeg

Zest of 3 oranges

Zest of 2 lemons

1½ cups all-purpose flour

2 tablespoons unsweetened cocoa powder

½ teaspoon kosher salt

6 tablespoons unsalted butter, at room temperature

¾ cup firmly packed light brown sugar

4 large eggs

1 teaspoon pure vanilla extract

1 cup semisweet chocolate chips

1. Preheat the oven to 350°F and line two large baking sheets with parchment paper. Place the hazelnuts, almonds, granulated sugar, cinnamon, cardamom, and nutmeg in a food processor and blitz until fine. Add the orange zest and lemon zest and blitz until incorporated. Set the mixture aside.

2. Place the flour, cocoa, and salt in a small bowl, and whisk to combine. Place the butter and brown sugar in a mixing bowl, and beat at medium speed with a handheld mixer fitted with the paddle attachment until pale and fluffy, scraping down the sides of the bowl as needed. Add the eggs and vanilla, reduce speed to low, and beat to incorporate. With the handheld mixer running at low speed, gradually add the flour mixture and beat until a smooth dough forms. Add the nut mixture and beat until incorporated.

3. Place 2-tablespoon portions of the dough on the baking sheets. Bake, rotating the sheets halfway through, for about 14 minutes, until the edges are set and the tops start to crack. Remove from the oven and let the cookies cool on the baking sheets.

4. Place the chocolate chips in a microwave-safe bowl, and microwave on medium until melted and smooth, removing to stir every 15 seconds. Spoon the melted chocolate over the cookies and let it set before serving.

KIPFERL BISCUITS

YIELD: 12 COOKIES | ACTIVE TIME: 40 MINUTES | TOTAL TIME: 2 HOURS

1⅓ cups all-purpose flour, plus more for dusting

½ cup unsweetened cocoa powder

½ teaspoon instant espresso powder

¼ teaspoon kosher salt

2 sticks unsalted butter, divided into tablespoons and at room temperature

¾ cup confectioners' sugar, sifted

¾ cup almond meal

1 teaspoon pure vanilla extract

½ cup white chocolate chips

1. Place all of the ingredients, except for the white chocolate chips, in a mixing bowl. Beat at medium speed with a handheld mixer fitted with the paddle attachment until a soft dough forms. Flatten the dough into a disk, cover it with plastic wrap, and refrigerate for 1 hour.

2. Preheat the oven to 350°F and line two large baking sheets with parchment paper. Remove the dough from the fridge and let it stand at room temperature for 5 minutes. Roll the dough into a ¾-inch-thick log, cut into 2-inch-long pieces, and roll them to form cylinders with your hands, while tapering and curling the ends to create crescent shapes. Place them on the baking sheets.

3. Bake for about 15 minutes, until set and firm. Remove from the oven and transfer the cookies to wire racks to cool.

4. Place the white chocolate chips in a microwave-safe bowl, and microwave on medium until melted and smooth, removing to stir every 15 seconds. Use a spoon to drizzle the melted white chocolate over the cooled biscuits and let it set before serving.

CHRISTMAS IN THE CARIBBEAN

YIELD: 36 COOKIES | ACTIVE TIME: 20 MINUTES | TOTAL TIME: 1 HOUR

3 tablespoons cream cheese, at room temperature

Zest and juice of 1 lime

1½ cups confectioners' sugar

2½ cups all-purpose flour

¾ cup caster sugar

¼ teaspoon kosher salt

2 sticks unsalted butter, divided into tablespoons and at room temperature

2 teaspoons pure vanilla extract

1½ cups sweetened shredded coconut, finely chopped

1. Preheat the oven to 350°F and line two baking sheets with parchment paper. Place 1 tablespoon of the cream cheese and 1 tablespoon of the lime juice in a mixing bowl, and stir until the mixture is smooth. Add the confectioners' sugar, and whisk until the mixture is smooth and thin, adding the remaining lime juice in 1-teaspoon increments until the glaze reaches the desired consistency. Set the glaze aside.

2. Place the flour, caster sugar, salt, and lime zest in a separate mixing bowl and whisk to combine. Add the butter one piece at a time, and use a pastry blender to work the mixture until it is a coarse meal. Add the vanilla and remaining cream cheese, and work the mixture until it is a smooth dough.

3. Form the mixture into balls and place them on the baking sheets. Bake until the cookies are a light brown, about 15 minutes. Remove from the oven and let cool to room temperature. Brush the glaze over the cookies and sprinkle the coconut on top. Let the glaze set before serving.

CHRUSCIKI

3 large eggs, at room temperature

¼ cup whole milk

¾ cup granulated sugar

1 stick unsalted butter

1 teaspoon baking soda

1 teaspoon pure vanilla extract

½ teaspoon kosher salt

½ teaspoon grated nutmeg

3½ cups all-purpose flour, plus more for dusting

Vegetable oil, for frying

1 cup confectioners' sugar, for dusting

1. Place the eggs, milk, granulated sugar, and butter in a mixing bowl. Beat with a hand-held mixer until thoroughly combined. Incorporate the baking soda, vanilla, salt, and nutmeg, and then add the flour. Mix until a soft dough forms, cover the bowl tightly with plastic wrap, and chill in the refrigerator for 1 hour.

2. Place the dough on a flour-dusted work surface and roll it out to ¼-inch thick. Cut into 1-inch-wide strips. Then cut the strips on a diagonal every 3 inches to form diamond-shaped cookies.

3. Add vegetable oil to a Dutch oven until it is 2 inches deep. Heat the oil to 375°F and add the cookies a few at a time. Use a slotted spoon to turn them as they brown. When cookies are browned all over, remove, set to drain on paper towels, and sprinkle with confectioners' sugar. Serve immediately.

GINGERBREAD MADELEINES

YIELD: 16 MADELEINES | ACTIVE TIME: 25 MINUTES | TOTAL TIME: 3 HOURS

5 tablespoons unsalted butter, plus more for the pan

½ cup gently packed brown sugar

2 eggs

1 tablespoon minced ginger

1¼ teaspoons pure vanilla extract

1½ tablespoons molasses

⅓ cup milk

½ cup all-purpose flour

½ cup cake flour

¼ teaspoon baking powder

1½ teaspoons kosher salt

¼ teaspoon ground cloves

¼ teaspoon grated nutmeg

1 teaspoon cinnamon

1. Place the butter in a small saucepan and cook over medium heat until lightly brown. Remove from heat and let cool to room temperature.

2. Place the butter and the brown sugar in a mixing bowl. Beat at medium speed with a handheld mixer fitted with the whisk attachment until light and fluffy. Incorporate the eggs one at a time, and then incorporate the ginger, vanilla, molasses, and milk.

3. Sift the flours and baking powder into a bowl. Add the salt, cloves, nutmeg, and cinnamon and stir to combine. With the mixer running on low, gradually add the dry mixture to the wet mixture and beat until a smooth dough forms. Transfer the dough to the refrigerator and chill for 2 hours.

4. Preheat the oven to 375°F and brush each shell-shaped depression in the madeleine pan with butter. Place the pan in the freezer for at least 10 minutes. Remove the pan from the freezer and the batter from the refrigerator. Fill each "shell" two-thirds of the way with batter and bake until a toothpick inserted into the center of a cookie comes out clean, about 12 minutes. Remove from the oven and place the cookies on a wire rack to cool slightly. Serve warm or at room temperature.

PFEFFERNÜSSE

YIELD: 24 COOKIES | ACTIVE TIME: 30 MINUTES | TOTAL TIME: 2 HOURS

2¼ cups all-purpose
flour, sifted

½ teaspoon kosher salt

½ teaspoon black
pepper

¼ teaspoon baking
soda

½ teaspoon cinnamon

¼ teaspoon ground
allspice

¼ teaspoon ground
nutmeg

1 pinch ground cloves

1 stick
unsalted butter, at
room temperature

1 cup firmly packed
light brown sugar

3 tablespoons
molasses, warmed

1 large egg

2¼ cups
confectioners' sugar

1. Place the flour, salt, pepper, baking soda, and ground spices in a large mixing bowl and whisk to combine. Place the butter, brown sugar, and molasses in a separate mixing bowl. Beat at medium speed with a handheld mixer fitted with the paddle attachment until pale and fluffy, scraping down the sides of the bowl as needed. Add the egg and beat to incorporate. With the handheld mixer running at low speed, gradually add the dry mixture to the wet mixture and beat until a smooth dough forms. Cover the dough in plastic wrap and refrigerate for 1 hour.

2. Preheat the oven to 350°F and line two baking sheets with parchment paper. Form tablespoons of the dough into rounded rectangles and place them on the baking sheets. Bake for 12 to 14 minutes, until the cookies are firm. Remove from the oven and transfer to wire racks to cool briefly.

3. Place the confectioners' sugar in a bowl and toss the cookies until completely coated. Place the cookies back on the wire racks to cool completely.

MEXICAN CHOCOLATE COOKIES

YIELD: 24 COOKIES | ACTIVE TIME: 20 MINUTES | TOTAL TIME: 40 MINUTES

1½ cups blanched almonds

3 cups confectioners' sugar

¾ cup unsweetened cocoa powder

1 teaspoon cinnamon

½ teaspoon kosher salt

1 cup bittersweet chocolate chips

4 large egg whites, at room temperature

½ teaspoon pure almond extract

1. Preheat the oven to 350°F and line two baking sheets with parchment paper. Place the almonds on another baking sheet and toast for 5 to 7 minutes. Reduce the oven temperature to 325°F.

2. Place the almonds and 1 cup of the confectioners' sugar in a food processor and blitz until the almonds are finely ground. Transfer the mixture to a mixing bowl, add the remaining sugar, the cocoa powder, cinnamon, and salt, and whisk to combine. Stir in the chocolate, egg whites, and almond extract, and work the mixture until it is a smooth dough.

3. Place tablespoons of the mixture on the baking sheets and bake for about 20 minutes, until the cookies are dry to the touch. Remove from the oven, and let the cookies cool on the baking sheets for 5 minutes before transferring them to wire racks to cool completely.

GLUTEN-FREE & VEGAN

Making everyone feel welcome and warmly embraced is a huge part of Christmas fulfilling its potential, and these cookies do exactly that. You can support them and delight their taste buds!

GLUTEN-FREE BUTTER COOKIES

YIELD: 24 COOKIES | ACTIVE TIME: 20 MINUTES | TOTAL TIME: 1 HOUR

⅓ cup almond meal

⅓ cup sorghum flour

½ cup rice flour

⅓ cup tapioca flour

½ cup cornmeal

⅔ cup granulated sugar

½ teaspoon guar gum

1 teaspoon gluten-free baking powder

Zest of 1 lemon

¾ teaspoon ground cardamom

1 pinch kosher salt

1 stick unsalted butter, chilled and diced

2 tablespoons water

1 large egg

½ teaspoon pure vanilla extract

2 cups confectioners' sugar

1 teaspoon fresh lemon juice

Hot water (125°F), as needed

Ground cardamom, for topping

Ground anise, for topping

1. Place the almond meal, flours, cornmeal, sugar, guar gum, baking powder, lemon zest, cardamom, and salt in a food processor and pulse to combine.

2. Add the butter and pulse until the mixture is coarse crumbs. Add the water, egg, and vanilla, and pulse until the mixture is just holding together. Cover the dough with plastic wrap and refrigerate for 30 minutes.

3. Preheat the oven to 350°F and line two baking sheets with parchment paper. Roll out the dough between two sheets of parchment paper and use cookie cutters to create the desired shapes.

4. Bake for 15 minutes, until a light golden brown. Remove from the oven and let cool on the baking sheets for a few minutes before transferring them to wire racks to cool completely.

5. Place the confectioners' sugar in a mixing bowl. Incorporate the lemon juice and enough hot water to give the frosting a thick consistency. Spread the frosting on the cookies or place it in a piping bag if a more decorative design is desired. When all of the cookies have been frosted, sprinkle the cardamom and anise over them.

GLUTEN-FREE CORNMEAL COOKIES

YIELD: 36 COOKIES | ACTIVE TIME: 15 MINUTES | TOTAL TIME: 40 MINUTES

¼ cup golden raisins

¼ cup dried cranberries

¼ cup dried cherries

¼ cup rum

1½ cups cornmeal

1½ cups cornstarch

¾ cup granulated sugar

1 teaspoon gluten-free baking powder

½ teaspoon xanthan gum

½ teaspoon kosher salt

1 stick unsalted butter, chopped

2 large eggs

2 tablespoons milk

Zest of 1 orange

½ teaspoon pure vanilla extract

1. Preheat the oven to 350°F and line two baking sheets with parchment paper. Place the dried fruits and rum in a mixing bowl and toss to coat.

2. Place the cornmeal, cornstarch, sugar, baking powder, xanthan gum, and salt in a food processor and pulse to combine. Add the butter and pulse until coarse crumbs form.

3. Place the eggs, milk, orange zest, and vanilla in a bowl, and whisk to combine. Add the mixture to the food processor and pulse until a stiff dough forms. Place the dough in a mixing bowl, add the rum-soaked dried fruit, and stir until evenly distributed. Form 1-tablespoon portions of the dough into balls and place them on the baking sheets.

4. Bake for 20 minutes, until the cookies are golden brown. Remove from the oven and briefly let cool on the baking sheets before transferring to a wire rack to cool completely.

GLUTEN-FREE CRANBERRY & NUT BARS

YIELD: 36 BARS | ACTIVE TIME: 20 MINUTES | TOTAL TIME: 45 MINUTES

¾ cup chopped walnuts

1 cup brown rice flour

⅓ cup potato starch

¼ cup tapioca starch

1 teaspoon gluten-free baking powder

¾ teaspoon xanthan gum

¼ teaspoon kosher salt

1 stick unsalted butter, at room temperature

1¼ cups firmly packed light brown sugar

2 large eggs

½ teaspoon pure vanilla extract

1 cup chopped fresh or frozen cranberries

1. Preheat the oven to 350°F and grease a 9-by-13-inch baking pan with nonstick cooking spray. Place the walnuts on a baking sheet, place it in the oven, and toast for 5 to 7 minutes. Remove from the oven and let cool.

2. Place the rice flour, potato starch, tapioca starch, baking powder, xanthan gum, and salt in a mixing bowl, and whisk to combine. Place the butter and brown sugar in a separate mixing bowl. Beat at medium speed with a handheld mixer fitted with the paddle attachment until light and fluffy, scraping down the sides of the bowl as needed. Incorporate the eggs one at a time, and then add the vanilla. Beat until incorporated. Gradually add the dry mixture and beat until the dough just holds together. Fold the walnuts and cranberries into the dough and then press it into the baking pan.

3. Bake for about 20 minutes, until the top is brown. Remove from the oven and let cool in the pan before cutting into bars.

GLUTEN-FREE GINGER FINGERS

YIELD: 24 COOKIES | ACTIVE TIME: 25 MINUTES | TOTAL TIME: 1 HOUR AND 45 MINUTES

2 cups brown rice flour

⅓ cup sweet rice flour, plus more for dusting

⅓ cup almond meal

1 teaspoon xanthan gum

½ teaspoon kosher salt

2 sticks unsalted butter, at room temperature

⅔ cup firmly packed light brown sugar

½ cup minced crystallized ginger

½ teaspoon pure vanilla extract

1. Place the brown rice flour, sweet rice flour, almond meal, xanthan gum, and salt in a mixing bowl and whisk to combine. Place the butter and brown sugar in a separate mixing bowl. Beat at medium speed with a handheld mixer fitted with the paddle attachment until pale and fluffy, scraping down the sides of the bowl as needed. Add the ginger and vanilla, reduce speed to low, and beat until incorporated. Gradually add the dry mixture and beat until a stiff dough forms. Shape the dough into a ball, cover with plastic wrap, and refrigerate for 1 hour.

2. Preheat the oven to 350°F and line two baking sheets with parchment paper. Dust a sheet of parchment paper and a rolling pin with sweet rice flour. Place the dough on the parchment paper and roll out to ½-inch thick. Cut the dough into rectangles that are 4-inches long and 1-inch wide and place them on the baking sheets.

3. Bake for about 12 minutes, until the edges are brown. Remove from the oven and let cool on the baking sheets for a few minutes before transferring them to wire racks to cool completely.

GLUTEN-FREE CHOCOLATE & HAZELNUT COOKIES

YIELD: 36 COOKIES | ACTIVE TIME: 20 MINUTES | TOTAL TIME: 40 MINUTES

1½ cups hazelnuts, skins removed

1¼ cups bittersweet chocolate chips

3 tablespoons unsalted butter

2 tablespoons brown rice flour

2 tablespoons unsweetened cocoa powder

1 tablespoon cornstarch

¼ teaspoon gluten-free baking powder

¼ teaspoon xanthan gum

¼ teaspoon kosher salt

2 large eggs

½ cup granulated sugar

2 tablespoons hazelnut-flavored liqueur

½ teaspoon pure vanilla extract

1 cup semisweet chocolate chips

1. Preheat the oven to 350°F and line two baking sheets with parchment paper. Place the hazelnuts on a separate baking sheet and toast for 5 to 7 minutes. Remove from the oven and let cool.

2. Place the bittersweet chocolate chips and butter in a microwave-safe bowl, and microwave on medium until melted and smooth, removing to stir every 15 seconds. Let the mixture cool slightly.

3. Place the rice flour, cocoa powder, cornstarch, baking powder, xanthan gum, and salt in a mixing bowl and whisk to combine. Place the eggs, sugar, liqueur, and vanilla in a separate mixing bowl. Beat at high speed with a handheld mixer fitted with the paddle attachment until combined. Add the melted chocolate, beat to incorporate, and then gradually incorporate the dry mixture. Fold in the hazelnuts and semisweet chocolate chips.

4. Form tablespoons of the dough into balls and place them on the baking sheets. Bake for 10 to 12 minutes, until they are dry to the touch. Remove from the oven and let them cool on the baking sheets for a few minutes before transferring the cookies to wire racks to cool completely.

GLUTEN-FREE & VEGAN

GLUTEN-FREE CASHEW MACAROONS

YIELD: 36 COOKIES | ACTIVE TIME: 15 MINUTES | TOTAL TIME: 30 MINUTES

2 cups raw cashews, plus more for topping

1¼ cups granulated sugar

2 large egg whites, at room temperature

1 pinch kosher salt

½ teaspoon pure vanilla extract

Colored sugars, for decoration

1. Preheat the oven to 350°F and line two baking sheets with parchment paper. Place the cashews and sugar in a food processor and blitz until finely ground. Add the egg whites, salt, and vanilla to the food processor and blitz until the mixture is thoroughly combined.

2. Form tablespoons of the dough into balls and roll them in the colored sugars. Place the cookies on the baking sheets and press a cashew in the center of each one.

3. Bake for 10 to 12 minutes, until lightly brown. Remove from the oven and let the cookies cool for 2 minutes on the baking sheets before transferring them to wire racks to cool completely.

GLUTEN-FREE FLORENTINES

YIELD: 60 COOKIES | ACTIVE TIME: 25 MINUTES | TOTAL TIME: 1 HOUR

1½ cups sliced almonds

2 tablespoons white rice flour

1 tablespoon cornstarch

⅛ teaspoon xanthan gum

¼ teaspoon kosher salt

¾ cup granulated sugar

2 tablespoons heavy cream

2 tablespoons light corn syrup

5 tablespoons unsalted butter

½ teaspoon pure vanilla extract

1 cup bittersweet chocolate chips

1. Combine almonds, rice flour, cornstarch, xanthan gum, and salt in a food processor and blitz until the mixture is fine. Transfer to a mixing bowl and set aside.

2. Place the sugar, cream, corn syrup, and butter in a small saucepan and bring to a boil over medium heat, stirring frequently to dissolve the sugar. Boil for 2 minutes, remove the pan from heat, and stir in the vanilla.

3. Pour the liquid over the almond mixture and stir to combine. Let cool for 30 minutes.

4. Preheat the oven to 350°F and line two baking sheets with parchment paper. Place rounded teaspoons of the dough on the baking sheets and bake for about 10 minutes, until golden brown. Remove from the oven and let the cookies cool for 2 minutes on the baking sheets before transferring them to wire racks to cool completely.

5. Place the chocolate chips in a microwave-safe bowl, and microwave on medium until melted and smooth, removing to stir every 15 seconds. Dip the edges of the cookies into the melted chocolate, place them back on the wire racks, and let the chocolate set before serving.

GLUTEN-FREE SNOWBALLS

YIELD: 36 COOKIES | ACTIVE TIME: 15 MINUTES | TOTAL TIME: 30 MINUTES

1 cup chopped pecans

1½ cups white rice flour

¼ cup potato starch

¼ cup sweet rice flour

½ teaspoon xanthan gum

½ teaspoon kosher salt

2 sticks unsalted butter

1½ cups confectioners' sugar

1 teaspoon pure vanilla extract

1. Preheat the oven to 350°F and line two baking sheets with parchment paper. Place the pecans on another baking sheet and toast for 5 to 7 minutes. Remove from the oven and let cool. Reduce the oven temperature to 325°F.

2. Place the rice flour, potato starch, sweet rice flour, xanthan gum, and salt in a mixing bowl and whisk until thoroughly combined.

3. Place the butter and 1 cup of the sugar in a mixing bowl, and beat at medium speed with a handheld mixer fitted with the paddle attachment until pale and fluffy, scraping down the sides of the bowl as needed. Add the vanilla and beat until incorporated. With the handheld mixer running at low speed, gradually incorporate the dry mixture and then fold in the pecans.

4. Place tablespoons of the dough on the baking sheets and bake for 15 minutes, until lightly browned. Remove from the oven and let the cookies cool for 2 minutes on the baking sheets.

5. Place the remaining confectioners' sugar in a shallow dish. Dip the tops of the cookies in the sugar and then transfer them to wire racks to cool completely.

GLUTEN-FREE ICED ALMOND WAFERS

YIELD: 80 COOKIES | ACTIVE TIME: 25 MINUTES | TOTAL TIME: 16 HOURS

9 tablespoons unsalted butter

½ cup caster sugar

¼ cup light corn syrup

1 tablespoon cinnamon

½ teaspoon baking soda

3½ cups chickpea flour

⅓ cup sweet rice flour

¼ cup minced almonds

2¾ cups confectioners' sugar

Water, as needed

Red food coloring, as needed

Red sugar pearls, for decoration

1. Place the butter, caster sugar, and corn syrup in a large saucepan. Bring to a boil, stirring until the sugar dissolves. Add the cinnamon and baking soda, and stir until the color changes to a lighter shade of brown. Remove the saucepan from heat and stir in the flours. Stir briskly until thoroughly combined, add the almonds, and let the mixture cool. When the dough is cool enough to handle, knead the mixture with your hands until a soft, smooth dough forms. Form the dough into a long log with a diameter that is about 2½ inches, cover with plastic wrap, and refrigerate overnight.

2. Preheat the oven to 350°F and line two or three baking sheets with parchment paper. Slice the log into ¼-inch-thick rounds and place them on the baking sheets.

3. Bake for 7 to 10 minutes, until golden brown. Remove from the oven and transfer the cookies to wire racks to cool completely.

4. Sift the confectioners' sugar into a mixing bowl and gradually incorporate water until the frosting achieves the desired consistency. Place one-third of the frosting in a separate

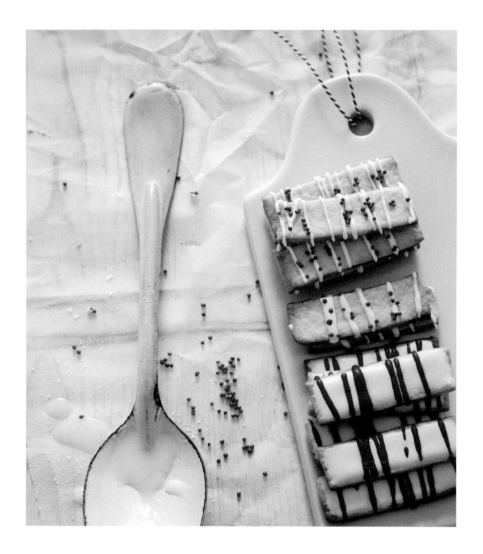

bowl, add food coloring, and stir to incorporate. Cover the red frosting with plastic wrap.

5. Spread the white frosting on the cookies and sprinkle the red sugar pearls over the top. Let the frosting set. Drizzle the red frosting over the white frosting and let it set before serving.

GLUTEN-FREE ALMOND & PINE NUT MACAROONS

YIELD: 36 COOKIES | ACTIVE TIME: 15 MINUTES | TOTAL TIME: 40 MINUTES

1 cup unsweetened
almond paste

1¼ cups granulated
sugar

2 large egg whites, at
room temperature

¾ cup pine nuts

1. Preheat the oven to 325°F and line two baking sheets with parchment paper. Break the almond paste into small pieces and place them in a mixing bowl along with the sugar. Beat at medium speed with a handheld mixer fitted with the paddle attachment until combined. Increase the speed to high, add the egg whites, and beat until mixture is light and fluffy.

2. Drop tablespoons of dough onto the prepared baking sheets. Pat pine nuts into tops of cookies. Bake for 18 to 20 minutes, until lightly browned. Remove from the oven and let the cookies cool on the baking sheets.

GLUTEN-FREE TEA COOKIES WITH LEMON GLAZE

YIELD: 24 COOKIES | ACTIVE TIME: 15 MINUTES | TOTAL TIME: 45 MINUTES

2 tablespoons loose-leaf Earl Grey tea

1½ cups granulated sugar

1 cup vegetable shortening

½ teaspoon pure vanilla extract

2 cups all-purpose flour, plus more for dusting

½ cup cornstarch

¼ teaspoon kosher salt

1½ cups confectioners' sugar

Zest and juice of 2 lemons

1. Preheat the oven to 350°F and line two baking sheets with parchment paper. Place the tea leaves and ½ cup of the granulated sugar in a food processor and blitz until combined. Transfer to a mixing bowl, add the remaining granulated sugar, shortening, and vanilla. Beat at medium speed with a handheld mixer until light and fluffy, scraping down the sides of the bowl as needed. Reduce the speed to low, add the flour, cornstarch, and salt, and beat until the dough holds together.

2. Place the dough on a flour-dusted work surface and roll it out to ¼-inch thick. Cut circles out of the dough and place them on the baking sheets.

3. Bake for 12 to 15 minutes, until the edges start to brown. Remove from the oven and let the cookies cool on the baking sheets.

4. Place the confectioners' sugar, lemon zest, and lemon juice in a bowl, and whisk to combine. Spread the glaze over the cookies and let it set for 15 minutes before serving.

GLUTEN-FREE PEANUT BUTTER COOKIES

YIELD: 24 TO 36 COOKIES | ACTIVE TIME: 20 MINUTES | TOTAL TIME: 35 MINUTES

1 cup brown rice flour

¼ cup tapioca flour

¼ cup cornstarch

1¼ teaspoons gluten-free baking powder

½ teaspoon xanthan gum

½ teaspoon kosher salt

1 stick unsalted butter, at room temperature

1 cup creamy peanut butter

½ cup granulated sugar

½ cup firmly packed dark brown sugar

1 large egg

1 large egg yolk

½ teaspoon pure vanilla extract

1. Preheat the oven to 375°F and line two baking sheets with parchment paper. Place the rice flour, tapioca flour, cornstarch, baking powder, xanthan gum, and salt in a mixing bowl, and whisk to combine.

2. Place the butter, peanut butter, and sugars in a mixing bowl, and beat at medium speed with a handheld mixer fitted with the paddle attachment until pale and fluffy, scraping down the sides of the bowl as needed. Add the egg, egg yolk, and vanilla, reduce speed to low, and beat to incorporate. With the handheld mixer running at low speed, gradually add the dry mixture to the wet mixture, and beat until a stiff dough forms.

3. Form tablespoons of the dough into balls and place them on the baking sheets. Flatten balls with the tines of a fork, making a crosshatch pattern on the top. Bake for 8 to 10 minutes, until golden brown. Remove from the oven and let the cookies cool on the baking sheets for 5 minutes before transferring them to wire racks to cool completely.

GLUTEN-FREE CANDIED CHERRY & WALNUT COOKIES

YIELD: 36 COOKIES | ACTIVE TIME: 20 MINUTES | TOTAL TIME: 50 MINUTES

1½ cups white rice flour

1 cup confectioners' sugar

½ cup cornstarch

1 teaspoon xanthan gum

1 teaspoon cream of tartar

1 pinch kosher salt

2 sticks unsalted butter, cut into thin slices

1 large egg

1 tablespoon milk

1 teaspoon pure vanilla extract

1 cup minced walnuts

18 red or green candied cherries, cut in half

1. Preheat the oven to 350°F and line two baking sheets with parchment paper. Place the rice flour, confectioners' sugar, cornstarch, xanthan gum, cream of tartar, and salt in a food processor, and blitz until combined. Add the butter and pulse until the mixture is coarse crumbs.

2. Place the egg, milk, and vanilla in a small cup, and whisk to combine. Drizzle the mixture into the food processor and pulse until a stiff dough forms. Place the walnuts on a sheet of waxed paper. Form tablespoons of the dough into balls, roll them in walnuts, and place them on the baking sheets. Make an indentation in the center of each ball with a finger and place one cherry piece in the indentation.

3. Bake for 12 to 14 minutes, until firm to the touch. Remove from the oven, and let the cookies cool on the baking sheets for 2 minutes before transferring them to wire racks to cool completely.

GLUTEN-FREE SUGAR COOKIES

YIELD: 36 COOKIES | ACTIVE TIME: 30 MINUTES | TOTAL TIME: 1 HOUR AND 45 MINUTES

1½ cups amaranth flour

2 cups confectioners' sugar

½ cup cornstarch

1 teaspoon xanthan gum

1 teaspoon cream of tartar

1 pinch kosher salt

2 sticks unsalted butter, cut into thin slices

1 large egg

1 tablespoon milk

1 teaspoon pure vanilla extract

Sweet rice flour, for dusting

Juice of 1 lemon

Colored sugars, for decoration

1. Combine amaranth flour, half of the confectioners' sugar, cornstarch, xanthan gum, cream of tartar, and salt in a food processor, and blitz until combined. Add the butter and pulse until the mixture is coarse crumbs.

2. Place the egg, milk, and vanilla in a small cup and whisk to combine. Drizzle the mixture into the food processor and pulse until a stiff dough forms. Divide the dough in half, cover each piece in plastic wrap, and flatten them into disks. Refrigerate for 1 hour.

3. Preheat the oven to 350°F and line two baking sheets with parchment paper. Lightly dust a sheet of waxed paper and a rolling pin with sweet rice flour. Place the dough on the paper and roll out to a ¼-inch thick. Use cookie cutters to cut the dough into desired shapes and place them on the baking sheets.

4. Bake for 10 to 12 minutes, until the edges start to brown. Remove from the oven, and let the cookies cool on the baking sheets for 5 minutes before transferring them to wire racks to cool completely.

5. Place the remaining confectioners' sugar and lemon juice in a mixing bowl, and stir until the icing has the desired consistency. Spread the icing on the cookies, sprinkle the colored sugars on top, and let set before serving.

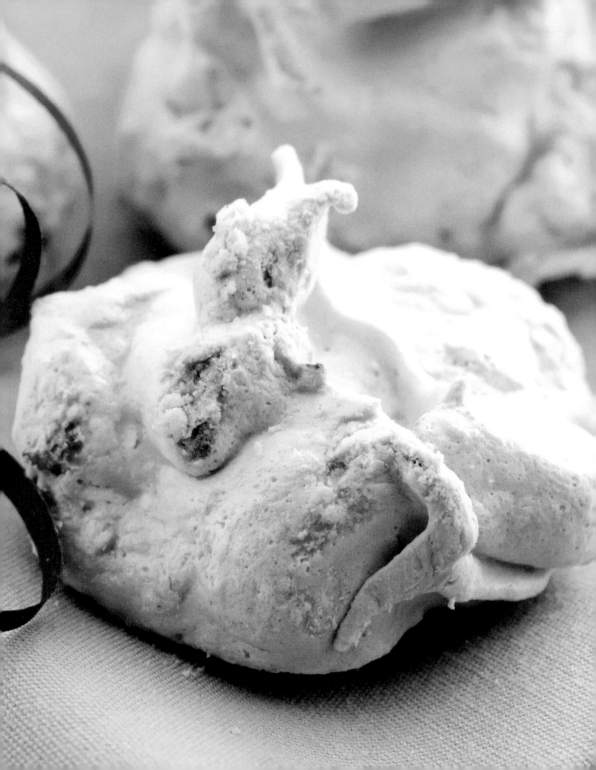

GLUTEN-FREE PRALINE MERINGUES

YIELD: 36 COOKIES | ACTIVE TIME: 20 MINUTES | TOTAL TIME: 1 HOUR AND 30 MINUTES

2 cups chopped pecans

5 large egg whites, at room temperature

⅓ teaspoon cream of tartar

¼ teaspoon kosher salt

1½ cups firmly packed dark brown sugar

½ teaspoon pure vanilla extract

1. Preheat the oven to 275°F and line two baking sheets with parchment paper. Place the pecans on another baking sheet and toast for 5 to 7 minutes. Remove from the oven and let cool completely.

2. Place the egg whites in a mixing bowl, and beat at medium speed with a handheld mixer fitted with the whisk attachment until frothy. Add the cream of tartar and salt, raise the speed to high, and beat until soft peaks form. Incorporate the brown sugar 1 tablespoon at a time and beat until stiff peaks form. Incorporate the vanilla and then fold in the toasted pecans.

3. Spoon the mixture into a piping bag fitted with a star-shaped tip. Pipe the mixture onto the baking sheets and bake for about 40 minutes, until dry to the touch. Turn off the oven, open the door, and let the meringues cool in the oven for 1 hour. Remove from the oven and transfer to wire racks to cool completely.

GLUTEN-FREE CORNFLAKE COOKIES

YIELD: 18 COOKIES | ACTIVE TIME: 30 MINUTES | TOTAL TIME: 1 HOUR AND 45 MINUTES

¾ cup caster sugar

1½ sticks unsalted butter, divided into tablespoons

7 tablespoons heavy cream

¼ cup honey

¾ cup sliced almonds

2 tablespoons cornstarch

3½ cups gluten-free cornflakes

Zest of 1 lemon

1 tablespoon chopped candied citrus peels

½ cup chopped candied cherries

⅔ cup raisins

1¼ cups dark chocolate chips

1¼ cups white chocolate chips

1. Preheat the oven to 350°F and line a baking sheet with parchment paper. Place the sugar, butter, cream, and honey in a large saucepan, and warm, while stirring, over medium heat until thoroughly combined. Remove the saucepan from heat, and stir in the almonds, cornstarch, cornflakes, lemon zest, mixed peel, cherries, and raisins. Let the mixture cool.

2. Place tablespoons of the batter onto the baking sheet and flatten them. Bake for about 10 minutes, until the top starts to brown. Remove from the oven, transfer to a wire rack, and let cool.

3. Place the dark chocolate chips in a microwave-safe bowl and microwave on medium until melted and smooth, removing to stir every 15 seconds. Repeat with the white chocolate chips. Dip half of the cookies in the dark chocolate, the other half in the white chocolate, and let them set before serving.

VEGAN OATMEAL COOKIES

YIELD: 48 COOKIES | ACTIVE TIME: 15 MINUTES | TOTAL TIME: 30 MINUTES

1 tablespoon egg
replacer

¼ cup cold water

⅓ cup vegetable
shortening

½ cup granulated
sugar

½ cup firmly packed
dark brown sugar

1 teaspoon pure
vanilla extract

1 teaspoon cinnamon

½ teaspoon baking
soda

1 pinch kosher salt

1 cup all-purpose flour

1¼ cups rolled oats

1 cup dried
cranberries

1 cup shelled and
chopped pistachios

1. Preheat the oven to 375°F and line two baking sheets with parchment paper. Place the egg replacer and cold water in a cup, stir to combine, and set aside. Place the shortening, granulated sugar, and brown sugar in a mixing bowl, and beat at low speed with a handheld mixer to combine. Increase the speed to medium and beat until light and fluffy, about 3 to 4 minutes.

2. Add the egg replacer mixture, vanilla, cinnamon, baking soda, and salt, and beat until thoroughly combined. Reduce the speed to low, add the flour, and beat until the dough just holds together. Add the oats, cranberries, and pistachios, and stir until combined.

3. Form tablespoons of the dough into balls and place them on the baking sheets. Bake the cookies for 12 minutes, until the edges are brown. Remove from the oven and let cool for 2 minutes on the baking sheets before transferring them to wire racks to cool completely.

VEGAN SNICKERDOODLES

YIELD: 30 COOKIES | ACTIVE TIME: 15 MINUTES | TOTAL TIME: 40 MINUTES

1 cup vegetable
shortening

1¼ cups granulated
sugar, plus 6
tablespoons

2 tablespoons oat milk

1 teaspoon pure
vanilla extract

1 cup all-purpose flour

⅔ cup whole wheat
pastry flour

2 tablespoons
cornstarch

1 teaspoon baking
powder

¼ teaspoon kosher salt

1 teaspoon cinnamon

¼ teaspoon grated
nutmeg

1. Preheat the oven to 350°F and line two baking sheets with parchment paper. Place the shortening, 1¼ cups sugar, oat milk, and vanilla in a mixing bowl, and beat at medium speed with a handheld mixer fitted with the paddle attachment until light and fluffy, scraping down the sides of the bowl as needed. Reduce the speed to low and incorporate the flours, cornstarch, baking powder, and salt. Beat until the dough just holds together.

2. Place the remaining sugar, cinnamon, and nutmeg in a small bowl, and stir to combine. Form tablespoons of the dough into balls, roll them in the sugar mixture until coated, and place them on the baking sheets.

3. Bake for 12 to 14 minutes, until the edges start to brown. Remove from the oven and let the cookies cool on the baking sheets for 2 minutes before transferring them to wire racks to cool completely.

VEGAN CRINKLE COOKIES

YIELD: 36 COOKIES | ACTIVE TIME: 20 MINUTES | TOTAL TIME: 45 MINUTES

2 tablespoons instant coffee grounds

2 tablespoons boiling water

½ cup vegetable shortening

2 cups confectioners' sugar

¼ cup silken tofu

½ teaspoon pure vanilla extract

¼ cup unsweetened cocoa powder

⅔ cup all-purpose flour

⅔ cup whole wheat pastry flour

1 pinch kosher salt

1. Preheat the oven to 350°F and line two baking sheets with parchment paper. Place the instant coffee and boiling water in a small bowl, and stir to dissolve the coffee. Let cool.

2. Place the shortening and ½ cup of the sugar in a mixing bowl. Beat at medium speed with a handheld mixer fitted with the paddle attachment until light and fluffy. Add the tofu and vanilla, and beat until incorporated. Add the cocoa powder and instant coffee, and beat until thoroughly incorporated. With the handheld mixer running at low speed, gradually add the flours and salt, and beat until the dough just holds together.

3. Form tablespoons of the dough into balls and place them on the baking sheets. Bake for 15 to 18 minutes, until firm and starting to crack. Remove from the oven and let the cookies cool on the baking sheets for 2 minutes. Sift the remaining confectioners' sugar into a shallow dish and roll the cookies in the sugar until coated. Transfer the cookies to wire racks to cool completely.

VEGAN FRUITCAKE COOKIES

YIELD: 24 COOKIES | ACTIVE TIME: 20 MINUTES | TOTAL TIME: 35 MINUTES

2 cups pecans

½ cup chopped dried apricots

½ cup chopped dried figs

1 cup chopped candied pineapple

1¼ cups all-purpose flour

½ cup vegetable shortening

½ cup granulated sugar

½ cup firmly packed light brown sugar

¼ cup silken tofu

1 teaspoon pure vanilla extract

½ teaspoon baking soda

½ teaspoon cinnamon

¼ teaspoon kosher salt

1. Preheat the oven to 350°F and line two baking sheets with parchment paper. Place the pecans on another baking sheet and toast for 5 to 7 minutes. Remove the pan from the oven and let the pecans cool briefly. Place them in a food processor and pulse until they are roughly chopped. Increase the oven temperature to 375°F.

2. Place the pecans, dried apricots, dried figs, and candied pineapple in a mixing bowl. Add ½ cup of the flour and toss to combine. Place the shortening, granulated sugar, and brown sugar in a separate large mixing bowl, and beat at medium speed with a handheld mixer fitted with the paddle attachment until light and fluffy, scraping down the sides of the bowl as needed. Add the tofu, vanilla, baking soda, cinnamon, and salt, and beat to incorporate. Reduce the speed to low, add the remaining flour, and beat until the dough just holds together. Fold in the nut-and-dried fruit mixture.

3. Form tablespoons of the dough into balls and place them on the baking sheets. Bake for 10 to 12 minutes, until the edges start to brown. Remove from the oven and let the cookies cool on the baking sheets for 2 minutes before transferring them to wire racks to cool completely.

VEGAN SPRITZ

YIELD: 96 COOKIES | ACTIVE TIME: 25 MINUTES | TOTAL TIME: 2 HOURS

1 tablespoon egg replacer

¼ cup cold water

1 cup vegetable shortening

⅔ cup granulated sugar

1 teaspoon pure vanilla extract

¼ teaspoon kosher salt

2½ cups all-purpose flour

Colored sugars, for decoration

Preferred candies, for decoration

1. Place the egg replacer and water in a cup, and whisk to combine. Place the shortening and sugar in a mixing bowl, and beat at medium speed with a handheld mixer fitted with the paddle attachment until pale and fluffy, scraping down the sides of the bowl as needed. Add the egg replacer mixture, vanilla, and salt, and beat until thoroughly incorporated. Gradually add the flour and beat until soft dough forms. Divide the dough in half, cover each half in plastic wrap, and flatten them. Refrigerate for 1 hour.

2. Preheat the oven to 350°F and line two baking sheets with parchment paper. Shape handfuls of the dough into logs, place them in a cookie press, and press them onto the baking sheets. Decorate cookies with the colored sugars and candies as desired.

3. Bake cookies for 12 to 15 minutes, until the edges are brown. Remove from the oven and let the cookies cool on the baking sheets for 2 minutes before transferring them to wire racks to cool completely.

VEGAN APRICOT BARS

YIELD: 48 BARS | ACTIVE TIME: 15 MINUTES | TOTAL TIME: 40 MINUTES

1½ cups sweetened shredded coconut

1 cup whole wheat pastry flour

½ cup all-purpose flour

1 cup firmly packed light brown sugar

¼ teaspoon kosher salt

¾ cup vegetable shortening

1 cup rolled oats

¾ cup apricot jam

¾ cup almonds

1. Preheat the oven to 375°F and grease a 9-by-13-inch baking pan with nonstick cooking spray. Place half of the coconut on a baking sheet and toast it in the oven for 6 to 8 minutes, until it starts to brown. Remove from the oven and let cool.

2. Place the flours, sugar, and salt in a food processor, and blitz to combine. Add the shortening and blitz until the mixture is coarse crumbs. Transfer the mixture to a mixing bowl, add the toasted coconut and oats, and use your hands to knead the mixture until a smooth dough forms.

3. Reserve ¾ cup dough and press the remaining dough into the bottom of the baking pan. Spread the jam over the dough, crumble the reserved dough on top of the jam, and sprinkle the remaining coconut over everything. Arrange the almonds on top in a decorative pattern.

4. Bake for about 20 minutes, until the top is golden brown. Remove from the oven and let cool in the pan before cutting into bars.

GLUTEN-FREE & VEGAN

INDEX

. . . .

METRIC CONVERSION CHART

U.S. Measurement	Approximate Metric Liquid Measurement	Approximate Metric Dry Measurement
1 teaspoon	5 ml	—
1 tablespoon or ½ ounce	15 ml	14 g
1 ounce or ⅛ cup	30 ml	29 g
¼ cup or 2 ounces	60 ml	57 g
⅓ cup	80 ml	—
½ cup or 4 ounces	120 ml	113 g
⅔ cup	160 ml	—
¾ cup or 6 ounces	180 ml	—
1 cup or 8 ounces or ½ pint	240 ml	227 g
1½ cups or 12 ounces	350 ml	—
2 cups or 1 pint or 16 ounces	475 ml	454 g
3 cups or 1½ pints	700 ml	—
4 cups or 2 pints or 1 quart	950 ml	—

ABOUT CIDER MILL PRESS BOOK PUBLISHERS

. . . .

Good ideas ripen with time. From seed to harvest, Cider Mill
Press brings fine reading, information, and entertainment
together between the covers of its creatively crafted books.
Our Cider Mill bears fruit twice a year, publishing a new crop
of titles each spring and fall.

"Where Good Books Are Ready for Press"

501 Nelson Place
Nashville, Tennessee 37214

cidermillpress.com